AF527792

DEVELOPMENT PRIORITIES IN NORTH-EAST INDIA

Books Published for NEICSSR, Shillong

Agenda for North East India — *B. Datta Ray*

Guwahati : The Gateway to the East — *A. Alam, N. C. Das* and *A. K. Borah (eds.)*

Population Poverty and Environment in North East India — *B. Datta Ray, H. K. Mazhari, P. M. Passah* and *N. C. Pandey (eds.)*

Reorganisation of North East India Since 1947 — *B. Datta Ray* and *S. P. Agrawal*

About the Editor

Bimal J. Deb is Professor of Political Science, North-Eastern Hill University. He is a former General Secretary of the North-East India Political Science Association. Currently he is also Hony. Secretary, Meghalaya Regional Branch of Indian Institute of Public Administration and Treasurer of North-East India Council for Social Science Research.

DEVELOPMENT PRIORITIES IN NORTH-EAST INDIA

Edited by

BIMAL J. DEB

CONCEPT PUBLISHING COMPANY, NEW DELHI-110059

All rights reserved. No part of this work may be reproduced, stored in a retrieval system, or transmitted in any form or by any means, electronic, mechanical, photocopying, microfilming, recording or otherwise, without the prior written permission of the copyright owner and the publisher.

The views and opinions expressed in this report are those of the authors and do not necessarily reflect the views of the organization to which they belong.

ISBN-81-7022-992-8

First Published 2002

© NEICSSR, Shillong

Published and Printed by
Ashok Kumar Mittal
Concept Publishing Company
A/15-16, Commercial Block, Mohan Garden,
NEW DELHI-110059

Phones : 5351460, 5351794
Fax : 091-11-5357103
E-mail : publishing@conceptpub.com

PREFACE

The twenty-first century has opened up spectacular opportunities in terms of acquisition of wide ranging new knowledge and scientific and technological advancements to be able to meet the crucial challenge facing North East India. Balance between economy and ecology depends on the working out of a healthy partnership between humans and nature. This calls for the existence of a truly democratic civil society that ensures economic efficiency and ecological harmony for total eradication of poverty and promotion of human welfare. We need a just political and social structure to ensure the participation of people in real terms in the decision making process at the different level of social and state structure. And also it is growingly realized that the civil society has a significant role to play in counterbalancing state absolutism. The civil society can be a bulwork against the onslaught of the multinational corporations. The surging wave of liberalisation, globalisation and privatisation has hit the social feeling giving rise to individualism and consumerism. Science and technology have opened up avenues assuring everyone food, health, education and home. We need an assurance of equity and social justice.

North East India has lagged behind in development despite its vast potentials. The untapped hydel power, mineral resources, virgin forests, sturdy people and water resources of the region could change the face of North East India. Lack of development has brought about a sense of neglect and frustration among people. Young people are feeling alienated and getting restless. There is thus an urgent need for the systematic analysis of the total issues involving balance between economy and ecology, population, human settlement pattern, physical resources and social justice.

We held in December 1999 a workshop on the occasion of the Silver Jubilee celebration of North East India Council for Social Science Research. The papers included in the volume were read in the workshop. We are grateful to His Excellency, Mr. M. M. Jacob, Governor of Meghalaya, who inaugurated the workshop. Anthropological Survey of India, Housing and Urban Development Corporation (HUDCO) and Indian Council of Social Science Research gave all the logistic support to the workshop on the 21st century and the Emerging Social Issues. We are thankful to everyone for help.

We would like to thank Mr. Ashok Kumar Mittal and the Concept

Publishing Company, New Delhi for undertaking the early publication of this volume. We thank also Dr. S. P. Agrawal, a former Director of Indian Council of Social Science Research, New Delhi for taking special interest in this publication.

B. Datta Ray
Shillong

Secretary,
North-East India Council for
Social Science Research

CONTENTS

LIST OF CONTRIBUTORS

Banerjee, Amalesh, Professor of Economics, Rabindra Bharati University, Calcutta.

Bhattacharjee, R. P., Assistant Registrar, NERIST, Nirjuli, Arunachal Pradesh.

Bhattacharyya, N. N., Formerly Professor of Economics, Gauhati University.

Borkakoti, S. K., A.D.P. College, Nagaon, Assam.

Borthakur, D. N., Former Vice-Chancellor, Assam Agricultural University, Jorhat.

Butola, B. S., Reader in Geography, J.N.U., New Delhi.

Chakravarty, D. N., Retd. Dean, Assam Agricultural University, Jorhat.

Deb, B. J., Professor of Political Science, North Eastern Hill University, Shillong.

Dutta, P. C., Economist, Assam.

Ganguli, J. B., Former Vice-Chancellor, Tripura University, Tripura.

Lahiri, T. B., Former Director, National Institute of Rural Development, Hyderabad.

Maiti, Asok Kumar, Professor of Economics, Indian Statistical Institute, Calcutta.

Mishra, A. K., Scientist, Soil and Water Conservation Engineering, I.C.A.R., Umiam, Meghalaya.

Mohapatra, A. C., Professor of Geography, N.E.H.U., Shillong.

Ray, Asok Kumar, Freelance Scholar.

Sarma, Kailash, Scholar, Nalbari, Assam.

Satapathy, K. K., Principal Scientist, ICAR, Umiam.

Upadhaya, N., Professor and Registrar, NERIST.

1

BACKGROUNDER

B. J. Deb

Development dialogue in North-East India admittedly hinges on tackling backlogs in basic minimum services and infrastructural needs. The fact however remains that development problems are compounded by insurgency and insecurity. While backwardness of the region stemmed from geo-political realities, militancy got its fillip from unprecedented ethnic mobilisations which sought legitimacy by being within the framework of politics but more through unconstitutional means. Although the question of central neglect is debatable, one fails to understand why its approach lacked uniformity and long term perspective.

Divergent approaches were formulated from time to time without any clear-cut sense of purpose. Some decisions taken were not even put into action. Created with the twin objectives of development and security, the North-Eastern Council remained a halfway house unable to make any dent whatsoever in either sphere. Instead of playing an advisory role in regional development, it became a mere funding agency, an unwitting platform of acrimony, bickering and mutual suspicion.

In the NEC every State was interested in getting its schemes approved oblivious of long-term interests. While Mizoram and Tripura persistently demanded equitable distribution of funds, Arunachal Pradesh did not see eye to eye with Assam on hydel projects. The term seven-sisters remains rhetoric — a euphemism used by politicians to fan emotions. The seven States of the region enjoy special category status to develop backward areas. They get preferential treatment in the matter of distribution of Central assistance bypassing the Gadgil formula which gives weightage to population, incidence of poverty and performance. Dilution of the formula meant plan assistance to the States to the extent of 90 per cent grant and 10 per cent loan. For the non-special category States the ratio is 30 : 70. Further, under the modified Gadgil formula Central plan assistance to special category States during the Eighth Plan was about 30 per cent of the total normal Central assistance. No less gratifying is the fact that the North-East with five per cent of the country's population has the highest per capita investment. Even then there is no perceptible development commensurate with the flow of money from the Central coffer. In the Union Rural Development Ministry's latest assessment there has been diversion of rural development funds to the militants which necessarily hampered rural upliftment. Time and again the Centre has made it known that development of the North-East is vital for tackling extremism or strengthening national security. The growth of extremist organisations, coupled with the ability of some of them to influence the process of legitimate politics and the alleged nexus of political parties with such forces, are undoubtedly impeding the development process.

This volume addresses the problems and constraints of development in the North-Eastern region, from multidimensional angles and outlines the priorities of today. Amalesh Banerjee in his *Development Dialogue* sets in motion contours of development and examines the contemporary social and economic institutions in India and their receptivity to economic change. Against this background, it was very appropriate that investment priorities in the North-East were properly examined. At the same time, the scholar underlines the need to organise public initiative to spur the Government into action. A.C. Mahapatra discusses rather convincingly several coexisting paradigms that explain underdevelopment in the region and pleads for a blue print of development based on internal capabilities and comparative advantages and achieve goals on a sustainable basis. Carrying the development discourse further, B.S. Butola examines the applicability of rational development paradigm to North-East Region and focuses in particular on nationalism and cultural development, development *versus* sustainable development, state *versus* civil society and power *versus* employment. Globalization, a catch word of today may not be a panacea for economic ills that confront us and hence A K. Maiti suggests adoption of abundant caution in seeking application of this trend. In a rather sceptical tone, he comes to the conclusion that regional and rational development would be shelved for all practical purposes in the current era of globalisation. J.B. Ganguli, on the other hand, is optimistic even though he refers to the UNDP findings that the process has not ensured the distribution of benefits evenly amongst nations and within nations. While pointing out the possible adverse impact of globalisation he suggests a new development paradigm stating that people of the North-East Region must have the liberty to decide what would be the appropriate technology for their productive enterprises and at what pace they would take advantage of the technological changes for improvement of their social, cultural and economic condition. The observation that civil society must play a vital role in ensuring effective participation of the people at the grassroots level in such a planning regime may indeed form the core of further developmental activities in the region.

Keeping civil society in the background of his conceptual analysis Asok Kumar Ray presents a case study on 'Assam Rural Infrastructure and Agricultural Services Projects' which is a World Bank sponsored project. According to the scholar, in the bandwagon of globalisation the tall claim of poverty alleviation as stated in the project document may not turn out to be sustainable.

The comprehensive review of natural resources of North-East India as a spring board for sustainable development in the twenty-first century has been presented in the book by A.K. Mishra in the context of worsening poverty and degradation of natural resources. A theoretically sound integrated development approach would be the best for natural resource management, environmental protection and overall well-being of the people of the region. The strategy suggested for natural resource management for sustainable development rightly puts emphasis on ensuring people's participation in natural resources conservation. The status of resource availability in the region is not disputed but it is all the more important to control forces which jeopardise resource sustainability. T.B. Lahiri presents an impressive analysis of the socio-economic parameters of the region on the basis of which he identifies priorities in social science research. In a more appropriate manner, the development scenario in the region is corroborated by N.N. Bhattacharyya with an emphasis on speedy and integrated development, although no particular strategy is put forward. The development dialogue continues with the presentation of its socio-economic perspective by Sanjib Kumar Borkakoti in which he pinpoints the need to rise above narrow sectarian interests and have a clear vision of the ideal type of society into which we want to transform ourselves. Any discussion on developmental issues in the North-East India is bound to be incomplete without taking into account the implications of shifting cultivation, a practice which continues to be so widespread in the hill areas of the region that all attempts at *jhum* control have proved to be inadequate. The crux of matter continues to be the control mechanism which alone could rejuvenate economy of the region and bring about improvements in the socio-economic condition of the people. This has been examined in detail by D.N. Borthakur giving a thrust on adoption of strategies aimed at providing a viable alternative to shifting cultivation.

A critical component of development of the North-East region is admittedly the human development indices and this view is presented by R.P. Bhattacharjee by taking a clue from Human Development index introduced by the UNDP in 1990. Equally important is the issue of population growth and environmental crisis in North-East India well explained rather convincingly by P.C. Dutta. This emphasis assumes importance specially because the planning efforts in India are directed to improve the standard of living and quality of life. Another paper entitled 'Population Growth and Demographic Balance' by Kailash Sarma discusses how the balance between different groups of people, whether ethnic, religious or linguistic, is disturbed.

Of late, Non-Governmental Organisations have come to occupy a distinct space in civil society. However political economy of the developing countries is full of contradictions and paradoxes which also limit the scope of NGO participation in the economic development. B.J. Deb examines the comparative advantages enjoyed by the NGOs even though the fact remains that they do not reach the poorest segment of the population especially in the rural areas. However, the rationale of bottom up approach for spreading the fruits of development is not disputed, although it is too early to say that NGO activism signifies the emergence of an alternative paradigm of social change. Sustainable development according to D.N. Chakravorty requires meeting the essential needs of all citizens and extending all opportunities to satisfy their aspirations for a better life. While stressing a sensible participation of people, he refers to an NGO working in the field of rural development in Assam which raised agricultural productivity considerably. In the same vein, K.K. Satapathy analyses the benefit of enlisting people's participation in soil conservation and watershed management programmes in the North-Eastern region. It has been rightly held that along with the introduction of innovative technologies, the use of indigenous knowledge and local innovations must be fostered and encouraged.

2

DEVELOPMENT DIALOGUE

Amalesh Banerjee

Development process of an economy is an outcome of collective effort of individuals and institutions in a society. It is the decision of individuals and institutions that determine the nature of product and the state of living of the people at large. Growth economists at the early stage, therefore, emphasised on institutions and values as important determinant of economic growth. Modern economists emphasising on endogenous growth therefore stress upon the development of group behaviour on institutional character. Improvement of institutional or group behaviour is a dynamic process that enhances the ethical and economic improvement.

There are two patterns of traditional group behaviour which have their modern version of collective decision. One line of thinking is the dictatorial process when the decision among the individuals for optimal solution of production and distribution become impossible. Arrow's impossibility theorem is a replica of that impasse and social welfare either hangs in balance or is directed by individual. History is replete with instances where economic and social progress was in this way directed for final solution. However, this process faces many obstacles at different stages and the situation is resolved either by abandoning the process and the programme or by putting down the alternative opinion. This way of resolving the development issues ultimately leads to stagnation. The other way of reaching the social optimality, is by expressing individual opinion by interaction and by making the social ranking. The institutional procedure to achieve this result is the democratic freedom. Social welfare and planning, therefore, has to be threshed out in a properly functioning peoples' forum. This democratic decision for social welfare, comprising production and distribution is a process of Pareto improvement and is the second best solution when the Pareto optimality is unavailable.

The basic issue of social dynamics is to admit of the vast diversity of human being and their widely different mode of expression depending upon their institutions, education and ethics. When there is wide diversity there is the necessity of a forum for admitting the opinion of groups or individuals consistent with that of others or not injurious to others. Such convergence of ideas produces important action for social change willingly agreeable to all. Take the case of fundamental of economic growth, the investment. From village community and city state to our modern states, investment decisions by community or planning forum is, by and large, based on individual and group decisions. However, when investments consistently ignore the welfare of the people, this invites resentment and desperation. In our discussion of development dialogue, we shall explore this point further. Before we go into that question one must remember the different interpretations of group decision — is it the group of poor, group of rich, or the ethnic group? However, all these melt down in a dynamic and dialectic dialogue of development.

Social Dynamics

Society has grown over historical process. In this process education, property relation and the culture arising out of that did play a crucial role. The usual explanation of this social formation is in terms of property relation. Where common property had been the basis of subsistence, the social formation has been formed around that which resembled some element of equity and justice of the primitive variety. However, this old village state has yielded place to village council where village administration is arrived at through democratic institutions. Old tribal societies and their property relations have undergone seachange under modern rules and regulations of the state. The old order of social fellow-feeling and community life has now given way to individualistic social relation. In place of social relation the earlier village chief oriented village administration has now given way to democratic village organisation. Whatever might have been the virtues of the old village life under the chief, it had died out yielding place to democratic institutions introduced by the state.

This old society with all its virtues has now undergone complete change in which old values might not be followed with equal degree of reverence as in the past. New administration, broader relation beyond the small valley and the impact of education and occupation on social life have acted as a strong dynamic force for transformation of the traditional culture of the tribal society.

Culture

Culture is a composite behaviour pattern of the human being which is given by many factors. Dynamics of cultural change is given by education, information, administration, besides the economic factors of income and social security. Culture undergoes change over time when these perspectives change. Education, information and contact with new mode of life and administration brought about vast changes in the age-old culture of the various traditional societies of north-eastern states. But the biggest contributory factor of those changes in culture are the economic factors. Take for example, the harvesting festival of many states particularly that of tribal society and also many other segments of society. However, changes of occupation and workforce structure brought about marked changes in the cultural part of life. Social life and dealings of the traditional society and for that matter in many other segments of society, are undergoing rapid changes under the impact of modern science and technological advance. In fact all culture types including folk society, feudal society and patrilineal bonds having special sociological socio-political, economic, technological and religious features have undergone rapid changes under modern scientific and technological innovation.

The evolution of cultural process is towards parallelism and convergence. As such the cultural relativism, the idea that every culture generates its own value system, is losing much of its edge. Under this universal evolution of social systems the dynamics of cultural diffusion in an integrated geographical limit of a country is all the more possible.

Against this natural porcess of an open society (and under modern scientific age every society is open through software connection) orthodox assertions is bound to be unacceptable. Recent experience of cultural revolution in China is a point to that effect. In a smaller scale, dogmatic assertions of religious groups are widespread in different parts of the globe. In historical lesson, we have seen, how the diverse cultural traits have undergone change in South Asian countries. Evolution from Indian cultures to Muslim and to European and a final adoption of cultural forces there, have been an example of cultural changes. Equally, without going into archaeological details, one can draw lessons from the South American Indians. Divided in innumerable groups and engaged in intense inter-tribal relations, the South American Indians became a part of the white civilization. These are only to remind us the nature of dynamics of culture taking from early days to our time in different parts of the world.

It is a lesson of how cultural dynamics of different society marches to modernity by continuous interaction of historical forces and gradual process of transformation and fertilization. It is the diffusion and interaction of different modes of culture that enliven the society and impart the essence of advance. Society leaps forward in this way otherwise being loaded with ossified obsequies of old traditions. As Satyajit Roy used to say and Amartya Sen recounts that, our culture can draw on 'their culture' as well, as can 'their culture' draw on ours. We indulge on this narration only to make an introspection as to what we have been doing in different parts of the country all in the name of purity of culture driving the people of an ethnic group from their hemlets by another ethnic group and trying to establish the might of one upon other. The caste war and the ethnic war are the two sides of the same coin of little egotism. Communitarians confine their attention to narrow bounds of particular community forgetting about the strength of assimilation. Arrogance brings annihilation of culture and accommodation widens it.

From pure anthropological to pure economic development, the relation is not far too distant. The institutions developed on the basis of socio-economic belief at one stage of historical process of a society must undergo change consistent with the dynamic forces going around in the structure of production and distribution. In fact, modern economic development again reverts to the importance of institutional chracter from the Harrodian technological model — from knife-edge to the institutional centre stage.

Growth economists, like Kaldor, placed emphasis on the growth rate of manufacturing sector. The growth of productivity is the important factor limiting the proportion of output and employment through expansion of manufacturing sector. But the degree of productivity growth was dependent both on the degree of institutional flexibility and the degree of institutional disruption. It is stated that the older the institutions, the less the receptiveness of the system. One reason of the British decline in the second-half of this century is that the productive and social structure of Britain remained untouched by big external shocks or discontinuities of two World Wars. In a predominantly agricultural economy which inherits immobile traditions and culture, rapid growth is presupposed by flexibility of social and economic institutions.

It is in this context that one will examine the contemporary social and economic institutions in India and their receptivity to economic change. One has to ask in how many states in India including NE states, the agrarian relations (and along with that the social relations) are receptive to agrarian reform? How is the institution of labour relations receptive to competitive development, as is prescribed by contemporary economic reform? For modern transformation of the traditional society, the ethnic relations and the economic relations must be flexible, not rigid, for advancement and welfare.

Investment

We earlier tried to introduce investment in the decision making process. We now revert to the point in a different type of social structure and ethnic stratification as stated above. Apart from intra-ethnic and inter-ethnic turmoil, there are other problems in the macrolevel development of the north-eastern states. Population explosion, either through high reproduction rate of the existing population or through migration of population from the neighbouring areas, is a problem. For example, Tripura is facing a population explosion; the case of Assam is no better. Most of the population is unskilled and untrained. Even for agriculture, the new surge of population is uninitiated to modern technique of cultivation. In the given context of the economic conditions of the NE states the factors of standard growth model of Horrodian type such as saving ratio, capital-output ratio and population growth rate do not show any consistency. Rising population, with limited natural resources, requires technological progress. Investment on an extensive scale for absorbing labour will increase output and employment.

The crux of the issue is that investment in manufacturing in extensive scale may not provide employment proportionately. The disequilibrium following from such investment creates dissension. This we have been doing over a long period of planning and development. The obsession with manufacturing expansion to the neglect of socially desired income and employment oriented activities resulted in structural imbalance. It has neither extended the export base of the economy nor laid the foundation of extended market within the economy. While at the early stage of planning Assam received oil refinaries and similar core industries but in the subsequent period downstream industries which would have provided larger employment, did not develop. Similarly investment in different tier in other states consistent with their resource base required priority consideration. Hence investment planning and technological adoption has to be socially planned in the forum of regional representatives of the people. Unfortunately, investment decisions in our country at present are in the hands of a band of triumvirate — the proprietary class, the bureaucrats and the politicians. The mutual interest of benefit, subsidies and black money have come to dominate the vital investment decisions for the benefit of a class. The employment and output generation are then channelised for the benefits of primarily the better off section of the population. The reform regime has not changed this basic defect of investment policy. The entire socio-economic and political structure has now developed a grand alliance. The unfortunate fact is that even in the recently developed states like Mizoram and Nagaiand the vital economic decisions and expenditures are being controlled by interested groups of people or the alliance mentioned. Modernity in these states has been fouled by collusive power brokers stated above. In proper economic development states like Mizoram, Meghalaya, Nagaland require innovative plan for investment for increased employment in productive economic activities and not merely in the tertiary sector. The importance of investment decision by the people lies in this case of determining the nature of investment.

Monetary Push

In the development process there is the tendency of depending upon money power rather than on real economic growth. Plethora of money is spent in the NE states without corresponding fundamental change in productive structures. In the north-eastern states, being in special category, Central Government fund flows, not always in proportion. This has resulted in demoralising the administration and the people. Money allocated for social welfare activities, partly goes to the poor but largely to the privileged few. Social values of dedication and commitment to the society has largely been eroded and is replaced by greed and personal aggrandisement. The socialising virtues of tribal society is yielding place to individual and self-seeking opportunism. Being in special category, almost the entire expenditure of these states is run by the Central Government. One result is that the people do not have to bear the corresponding cost of the benefit they are enjoying. State governments, on the other hand, have very limited financial strength. State revenue being very low, the state government expenditure, mainly on administrative purpose, is met by Central fund. The easy money thus flowing in the state has also made the state administrative sector almost parasitic and inefficient.

Money is having no relation with production or consumption. Or one can say, money is neutral to production. The irony is that money is not neutral in a growing economy but we have made it so. The real side of the economy being unresponsive or being bypassed, money is rolling to swell in the hand of undeserving people.

Dissent and Destruction

Disagreement and dissent has an important role in the development process. Disagreement, on the ground of principle, is a healthy process of development. However, if the objective of dissent is positive, it encourages the individuals and the institutions to take positive step to drive home the authority for correction of omission and commission. Destruction, however is the total denial of positive content. It is a pity that a large number of development activities in Assam, Tripura and other NE states are suspended due to destructive dissent. That such dissent is a blind alley is self-evident. Health, education and public utility services, important public enterprises and even festivities are crippled by violence and insurgency. Insurgency is not an expression of disagreement. It is a deliberate attempt to destroy the existing fabric of social and economic structure by blackmail, terror and annihilation. However, this is a total negation of democratic dissent. In a democratic structure this sort of violence did never pay in the past, and could not be so in the future. There are multiple origins of insurgency, (a) agency aspect, (b) oppression and (c) advantage aspect. Government has to take strong measures to contain all these origins. Foreign instigated insurgency has to be controlled by the state. In doing that states must also take necessary measures to curb the exploitation of workers and the ethnic groups.

Dissent, Democracy and Development

As stated above, dissent and opposition is the lifeline of democracy. Development programme initiated by an elected government may not be entirely beneficial to all segments of the population. Even the development programme may be partial and motivated for group interest, when the authority must be made to mend the ways. Dissent has an important role in these cases of democratic system to set the process in the right direction. As Sen and Dreze (1995) pointed out, both the state and public action have important role in economic development. There is a complementary relationship between the two. In a democratic development process public inaction and government apathy may create vicious circle of stagnation or even retardation. Organised public action will spur the government into action.

This dialectic process of complementarity between public action and government action make the society to progress and achieve economic development. Fury is important and often essential on the part of the disadvantaged section of the society for generating activism in the system, in administrative machinery and the productive system. But the target is essential for the human being and not annihilating him. Democratic development, therefore, has a great advantage of dynamic transformation through dialectic process.

There is a great possibility of the development of the NE states. The energy of the insurgent segments has to accommodate other segments in order to bring about a radical change in the development of the region. Suffering of the disadvantaged people is abysmal. A collaborative action is urgent to usher in a new era of prosperity, equality and welfare of the people of the North East.

REFERENCES

Bardhan, P. (1984). *The Political Economic Development of India.* Oxford University Press, Delhi.

Chakraborty, S. (1987) *Development Planning,* Oxford University Press.

Dreze, Jean; Sen, Amartya (1995) *India : Economic Development and Social Opportunity.* Oxford University Press, Oxford, New York.

Encyclopaedia Britannica (1982) Fifteenth Edition (USA), University of Chicago, Vol. 17: 223-274, Vol. 3:287.

Hodgson, Geoff (1989) 'Institutional Rigidities and Economic Growth' in *Cambridge Journal of Economics.* Vol. 13, No.1.

Sen, Amartya (1995) Lecture delivered at Nandan. Calcutta in Memory of Satyajit Roy, December 22, printed in *The Telegraph,* Calcutta, on January 1 and 2, 1996.

Solow, R.M. (1970) *Growth Theory,* Oxford University Press, London.

3

DEVELOPMENT AND UNDERDEVELOPMENT OF THE NORTH-EAST REGION : Search for a Paradigm

A. C. Mohapatra

The Nort-East region, 'the land of the seven sisters' is a morass of economic backwardness — it certainly does not deserve to be so. Pandit Nehru stated during the debate on the First Five Year Plan :

> "... It is admitted that there should be attempt to make every region, every part of India develop equally in so far as we can, and that we should remove the disparities that exist in India. There are some tremendous disparities. Some of our provinces, I would not name them are extremely poor. They do not deserve to be poor."[1]

The economic backwardness of the region owes partly to its chequered history — its colonial history, integration with the Indian nation; partly due to the fact of it being part of a large and poor nation, and also the fact of its geographical and economic isolation from the rest of the country. Much have been said and debated on woes of the region. The intention of this chapter is in a sense to summarise the main thrusts of the arguments about the backwardness of the region and develop perhaps, a new perspective.

The Colonial Perspective

North-East has been for ages, home of a large number of tribes and communities living in relative isolation in their own cultural and ecological niches, with the possible exception of the people in the great valleys of the region. They were, largely autonomous and had their own ways of social and economic organisation — that in some cases rivalled some of the best modern practices. The British came formally in 1826. The process of the region's incorporation into the Empire commenced. Two aspects of this development were significant. First, the region was brought under a single administrative umbrella, thus, some integration of the region into a single entity, though subjugation of many distant and interior territories continued for more than half a century thereafter. Second, it was not the interest of the people but the natural resources that became the focus of activities, especially those that served direct interests of the colonial masters — oil, tea and timber, to illustrate the point. This (latter) aspect has been possible responsible for a framework of development of the region that essentially became detrimental to interests of the people and more generally to the region as whole, because it promote a policy of turning the region as a *development frontier*.

Developments during the Early (Post-Independence) Decades

From the national perspective, the early two decades were decades of consolidation of the nation, both socially as well as economically. It was also a period of great difficulties particularly in respect of resettling post-partition displacements, food shortages as well as the three wars that the country had to fight that sapped the vitals of our economy. However, the colonial perspective of North-East region as a development frontier remained in all approaches to development programmes in the region during the period. The consequences of adherence to such a framework were the following :

1. The region was promoted as one with "tremendous" quantity of natural resources — a position not supported by facts. When 'industrialisation' was the buzzword of development agenda in fifties and sixties, natural resources meant essentially mineral resources. Such mineral resources barring mineral oil are scanty in the region. Mineral oil incidence in the region is limited and has been under commercial exploitation from the Digboi days (1874). There has been no fresh major finds after the sixties and the productivity of wells have declined substantially (right from the seventies). From a peak of over 5 mn tonnes, it has declined to less than 3 mn tonnes in recent decades. The commercially exploitable life is no more than 25 to 30 years. There is some incidence of tertiary coal in the region, but in the absence of suitable metallic minerals there is little potential for metallurgical industries in the region.

   The region is well endowed with hydroelectric potential. But it is a transient resource, in the sense that it has to be continuously harnessed and used — it cannot be stored up for future uses nor can it be effectively exported outside the region and traded.[2] Forests are people's resource. Though the region is well endowed with forests, even if large tracts of prime forests are lost, no big industrialisation can be based on such a resource without jeopardising livelihood systems of the people. This unfortunately, is something happening in recent decades in the region, endangering the forest systems and the environment, as well as the livelihood systems of the people.

The whole idea of lthe region's riches in natural resources (in the context as above) is untenable and has done more harms than good to the region. In fact, the natural resource systems of the region are quite fragile and need careful management while utilising them.

2. This framework also led to the "culture of carpetbaggers". A comparison of the situation can be drawn with what happened in the westward movement in the United States, especially after the railway-network expanded. On the extending western frontiers came townships of land-grabbers, carpetbaggers, new townships along the fresh laid railway lines, prostitutes and pimps, the ránches and cowboys, and concomitant to that the destruction of the Indians and their civilisation. The indigenous people and their culture were decimated to oblivion. An interesting economic interpretation was by Douglas North's monumental work on the Economic History of America.[3] North argued that the extending frontier of the US that was undeveloped, quickly started developing based on initially exporting primary products, like minerals, timber and agro-products etc. and started quickly industrialising since it could attract investments. Much that this view contains wisdom, he totally ignored the destruction of the people living there — the Indians, their civilisation and culture. That cost was enormous but was totally ignored by the forward march of capitalism into the heartland of the America.

   Those who promote, even if indirectly such a framework of development of the region would be at great peril to view the consequences of such a process in the North-East. The question of a *development frontier* and development based on export of primary commodities (natural resources) is to be thrown out of the window, totally rejected.

The Internal Colony Framework

The other important vantage through which the underdevelopment of the

North-East region is viewed is the "dependency framework" and its application in the national scale. The dependency framework that was developed during the mid-sixties and seventies by a host of scholars was put under the umbrella of "Latin American Theorists".[4] The attempt was to understand the global problematic of underdevelopment that despite two decades of *reconstruction and aid* seemed nowhere waning. Authors like Amin and Wallerstein consistently agrued that four centuries of colonial rule and direct exploitation and post-liberation dependence of these economies on the "world market" and consequent "value transfer" from the poor to the rich nations is what is principally responsible for underdevelopment of these countries — a "corollary to development in the developed nations". Foreign aid, instead of bringing socour to these nations have become root cause of all their woes — making them more and more dependent and enslaving their productive capacities to the vagaries of the world market. Some theorists have tried to explain economic underdevelopment within large countries using the dependency framework. In the same manner that advancing capitalism made it, in a sense, a historical necessity colonial expansion, turning the new areas (colonies) as peripheries supplying raw materials and in turn receiving finished goods and services. Large countries like India that emerged at the dawn of the post-colonial era turned their backward areas as peripheries — an internal colony to advancing industrial capitalism. The North-East region or the mineral rich central Indian territiories may well fit into this framework. Just as the dependency theorists could hardly provide an alternative to the existing global arrangement, except arguing for a more equal relationship between the North and the South, internal colony theorists have hardly an alternative to the *status quo,* the nation state. Those who argue for autonomy or outright independence have not demonstrated to any extent, if after decades and centuries (Latin America, for example) of political independence, more than a hundred developing countries have not come out of the morass of underdevelopment and poverty, how for example, even if granted political independence, the development of these backward, peripheral regions of the country could be guaranteed? On the other hand, at global scale, if foreign aid is seen as an instrument of furtherance of dependence, there is greater demand for larger aid to the backward regions — that by the same logic would further shackle them to economic dependence in perpetuity. Socialistic enterprise has failed globally as an alternative to industrial capitalism. There apears no alternative to the system of the "nations state". Some resolution is to be sought within the existing arrangement, perhaps till such time that viable method of social re-engineering is designed.

Regional Integration, Globalisation and Trade Framework

In the early nineties the Indian economy and polity started discarding its quasi-autarky and moved towards a liberalised economy with an outward looking perspective — globalisation. Foreign participation and investments in the Indian economy were welcomed with emphasis on external trade, currency float and internal economic reforms including loosening the Government's grip on industry and a host of other measures. The North-East region has great geographical isolation from the rest of the country, especially after independence and the partition. This had and has a telling effect on its economy, particularly competitiveness of its products and services due to high transport cost and time taken for products to reach markets elsewhere. Whereas this region remained cut-off and backward, in the vicinity there have been great happenings — great economic changes that have quickly come to Thailand, Malaysia, Singapore and Indonesia due to precisely outward looking liberalised economic policies in the last two decades. This region lies in much closer proximity to the North-East, much closer than many parts of India. If communication and external trade is promoted and appropriate physical linkages are developed with this fast developing region, the region can benefit immensely.[5] This is an extremely important, viable and pragmatic suggestion. With improvements in relationship with neighbouring countries like Bangladesh, Nepal and Myanmar some border trade has commenced. This is not enough. What is genuinely needed is the suggested super-highway through Myanmar to the economic powerhouse of Southeast Asia.[6] This is a long process and might take years to mature — much depends on the circumstances in Myanmar. However, many preparatory moves are needed from the Indian end in any case, and these could be initiated without delay. Such a move also requires safeguarding India's strategic interests — opening of the borders have its flip side too. In any case, under a liberalised dispensation, this ought to be part of a long-term strategy that truly can metamorphose the economy of the North-East.

An Alternative Internal Development Strategy

A long-term strategy of development of the region would be meaningless unless region prepares itself for such economic integration with the neighbouring economies. Its internal preparedness is crucial for benefits from mutual trade and travels. In the beginning it has been pointed out that the whole understanding of North-East's resource complex is misplaced that needs reassessment. Without such a review it may not be feasible to make important strategic internal changes. What construes the natural resources of the region? It has land, both fertile valleys and hills and forested tracts of immense beauty. It has water both, flowing — plenty of it, and the potential hydropower resources. It has people with their variegated cultures, skills and generally, a highly literate pool of manpower that is little used because of lack of employment oportunities. It has the forests and the biological (and genetic) resource pool. The resource complex, therefore, is not the dead minerals but *a living pool of resources.* Its development strategy must therefore be based on this living complex of resources, not necessarily industrialisation understood in the common parlance. It is not meant here that other industries like oil and petro-chemicals or coal or limestone based industries are to be discouraged. It is more in changing the emphasis on the direction of development. It would need a *new blue-print,* some of that is as follows:

(a) A strategic shift in emphasis in agriculture (crop farming) in the valleys from monsoon based practices (which may continue) to irrigation based farming during the off seasons. This region has one of the least irrigated areas of the country, since the traditional monsoon farming was considered adequate — irrigation was not promoted. From the farmers' point of view, monsoon not only provides water for the rice paddies; it also brings in the floods and the concomitant risks on investments. Flood protection though is necessary, it neither can be effectively controlled in the same manner as in other areas of the country, nor is desirable due to the sheer volume of discharge from the region. An effective alternative appears is the dry-season farming. This of course, needs substantial public investments as well as promoting private investments in irrigation. Agriculture can then yield a livelihood and may absorb a good proportion of the idle manpower.

The region is currently food deficit. If farming practices, crop calendar are changed enabled by irrigation, in a decade's time the region can turn the corner and become food surplus. But it may not gain comparative advantage *vis-a-vis* other grain farming areas of the country due to high transportation costs. This is when opening of links with neighbouring region of the Southeast Asia will come handy. However, rice will not enjoy a comparative advantage in those regions that already are surplus (Thailand and Myanmar, *e.g.*) and are technologically superior and more efficient. A change in product mix will be necessary. Trade and travel will bring in demonstration effect on the farming practices, since the agro-climatic conditions of North-East is much closer to the Southeast Asia than mainland India and thus, farming practices and technologies of that region will be more effective in North-East than the current practices promoted.

(b) In the hills, however, the strategy need not be grain farming, but a complex of silviculture, horticulture and animal husbandry, which wherever initiated have yielded excellent results.

(c) There must be accentuated research and development of plant-genetic resources of the region and promotion of economic species at the field level. This also needs appropriated documentation and patenting of genetic resources.

(d) The region also needs re-working of its manpower development from general education to professional and vocational programmes and skill upgradation programmes including farmers training for the suggested package strategy. Though a good literacy situation is an adequate starting point, it may not be enough without appropriate filtering of skills right down to the grassroot level.

(e) The region ought to promote its natural and cultural heritage as a marketable product. This again requires public and private investments in tourism development and skill upgradations in tourist services. The region can also promote its traditional products like cottage textiles with their wonderful designs and motifs as exportable commodities. Specialised designing and training centres will be essential. Though this is being done to some extent now, it is not enough and more specialised inputs and governmental support may be necessary.[7]

(f) There would be also the need for internal liberalisation within the region before any external integration is thought of.[8] External integration would require free movement, investment decisions and property ownership. Under the current liberalisation strategy and industrial promotion programmes in the region (tax holiday, for example) hardly any investment has flowed into the region principally because there are any number of restrictive laws prevalent. Investors abhor restrictions on their decision to invest — where to invest and what to invest. Without internal liberalisation, external integration and export promotion will remain a distant dream.

Conclusion

North-East is pregnant with possibilities. Its path to development and economic prosperity to a large extent lies in reworking its development strategy into areas it has comparative advantage and to the extent it is willing to liberalise internally and integrate with the national as well as international economy. The periodic doles from the Central Government alone (which may continue, in any case) may not do the job of catapulting the region to a higher level of development. Its hesitance to anything external may be its undoing. Economic strength provides a boost to culture and its promotion — a cultural cocoon has a short life. The choice is to be with the people — whether a more liberal, integrative outlook on development or an inward looking perspective that may keep the region in the morass of backwardness, poverty and unemployment. If an inward looking autarky like Japan could break open (1858)[9] and become a superpower in no time, why the North-East cannot become prosperous? *It has the means — it needs the will.*

NOTES

1. J. Nehru (1952), Parliamentary Debate on the *First Five Year Plan,* PC, Government of India.
2. A. C. Mohapatra (1992), "Zonal Planning in Power Development", *Planning Perspectives for the North Eastern and Eastern Zone,* Malcom S. Adiseshiah (ed.), Lancer Pub. Pvt. Ltd., New Delhi, 1992, pp. 25-46.
3. Douglas C. North (1933), *An Economic History of the United States of America.* North was awarded the Nobel Prize in Economics for lifetime work in 1992.
4. A large number of scholars contributed to this debate, principally Andre Gunder Frank, I. Wallerstein, Samir Amin, C. Furtardo and among Indian scholars R. Sau, M. Raza, B. Chattopadhyay, A. H. Kidwai.
5. B. G. Verghese, (1996), *India's Northeast Resurgent,* Konark Publishers Pvt. Ltd., New Delhi, (Chap. 16).
6. S. P. Shukla (1997), *Transforming the Northeast,* High Level Commission Report to the Prime Minister, Planning Commission, New Delhi.
7. China for example, exports handmade toys worth US $ 5 billion a year to western nations.
8. A. C. Mohapatra (1996), "Marketing, Gobal Integration and Development Scenario for Developing Countries with Specific Reference to India.", *Proc. of International Seminar of Marketing and Development,* Saitama University Japan, Dr. Kazuo Usui (ed.), Faculty of Economics, Saitama University, Japan, 1996, pp. 113-124.
9. Japanese economy was forced open by American gun boat diplomacy in 1858. By 1905 Japan has emerged as a major world power and could defeat the Tsarist Russia in Eastern Siberia and China in Manchuria.

4

DEVELOPMENT DISCOURSES IN SOCIAL SCIENCE RESEARCH IN THE NORTH-EASTERN REGION

B. S. Butola

India, the motherland of over one thousand million people, ever ready to defend its territorial integrity and political sovereignty even at the cost of their own lives is a construction based on one's opinion and ideological positions rather than an objective fact of history. One is right in saying that its objectivity is a matter of invention rather than of discovery[1]. It is a debatable issue to ascertain when its present identity came into existence and what will be the nature of its identity in the future. However, most scholars believe that the exact nature of the present construction of India came into existence some time in the mid-19th century with the growth of British Finance Capitalism and Imperialism. It was the imperative of the Finance Capital to create a unified and consistent cartographic image of India[2] for the purpose of resource inventory, investment spaces, market expansion and ultimately territorial expansion of the colonial empire into the other neighbouring territories. To undertake this gigantic yet the most significant task from the point of view of the future of British Empire in India, James Rennell's extensive survey in Bengal in 1760s provided the initial framework and later on it was formalised with the establishment of the Great Trigonometrically Survey in 1817. This was finally developed into the Organization of the Atlas of India in 1820s. The mission went uninterrupted for the years to come. The British imperialism continued to prosper at a very high human and environmental cost in the colonies. It was all done in the name of development.

Imperialism as Development

There were some important seminal transformation in the nature and the role of the British Imperialism in India. The business interests that were commenced with the opening of the office of East India Company in 1600 AD hereafter became a thing of the past and the British in their new incarnation particularly after 1757 had been aspiring for the total control and possession of the entire Indian subcontinent. The North-Eastern Region of India that had so far remained untouched from the influences of the world market and also of the British imperialism was the first to face the music in the 1820s. To begin with introduction of world famous tea plantation and construction of railways was done at the war footing in the region. Alienation of the local tribal inhabitants from their land and displacement of the indigenous tribal communities particularly from the central Indian tribal belts and their forceful settlement in the region was the saga of unprecedented agonies and worries to these uprooted people. The plantations became the economic and socio-cultural enclaves as far as the North-Eastern Region is concerned.

Moreover, the fall of the Delhi rulers and the victory of the colonial powers in 1857, added new impetus to this mission. It witnessed an unholy consummation of territory and knowledge for the benefits of the British Imperialism. India and millions of its people along with their rich and varied cultures, identities and spatial diversities became the target of new Imperial Social Engineering, exploitation, experimentation and manipulations. Thereafter, it was imperative to the imperialist to know a country in its all details in order to govern it. To achieve this end the maps prepared by them had clear reflections of their imperialist design. Many a place so far unnamed were assigned new identities. Most often, it happened by negating and annihilating the existing identities. Furthermore, while mapping the culture, social and economic diversities in India, the colonial rulers exhibited their economic interests and racial superiority over the Indians. The culture and civilisation that had survived and prospered over thousands of years and experienced the First Enlightenment of human hisotry in the 6th century BC and witnessed a series of social movements and upheavals was reconstructed in the image of the Imperialist. India the land of riches became a country full of squalor, inhabited by magicians and snake charmers. It became a country that has frozen in time without any sense of change and history. Thus, the colonial power took this responsibility upon them to civilise, aculturise, modernise and democratise the half animal half human nature of the Indian inhabitants. Their claims were strengthened and rationalised in the form of superior survey as well as production techniques and their ability to create knowledge, and of course the superior fire arms was not less significant. In the process, the particular and the unique that India had in abundance were sacrificed at the altar of the universal may it be the language, script, religion, cuisine, dress, architecture and even the social customs. It was the beginning of the age of celebrations of new ruling class equations: *"the universal — the rational and the developed"* against the *"archaic — the superstitious and the undemocratic"*.

Thus, the ideology of Map Making and the use of scientific technology also contributed in the construction of the "Other". This was the non-British, non-European and the Colonial. Now, the colonised was the "dreamy imagination" of the past, against the practical and the rational coloniser of the present. The "other" was considered simple, unchanging and incapable of progress and change without the generosity of the coherent, disciplined, orderly, enlightened and rartional coloniser. Moreover, the colonisers were firm in their opinion that for an efficient governance (apparently) and exploitation (in reality) a rational and orderly space can be managed only through a rational and orderly manner. It was so confusing to many scholars that they mistook this for process of modernisation and development. But, what was considered rational by the protagonist of world capitalism in general and the British imperialist in particular was nothing but, irrational and inhuman to the people of India. The so called generous approach of the coloniser towards the colonised in the name of development, democratisation and civilisation became the new *mantras* for spreading colonialism, exploitation and estrangement. However, the efforts of the colonial powers to recruit the indigenous people to run the colonial administration at the lower level was responsible in the formation of an army of middlemen, lower level administrators and middle classes. A large number of these always remained subservient to their colonial masters but, a tiny minority of these did voice their resentment and opposition to the British rule. Their exposure to liberal democratic values of the west and bewitched by the overpowering magic of the enlightenment rationality and the logic of modernity helped them to critically understand the mechanism of world imperialism. This class of people thus bcame aware of the increasing social disparities and discriminatory and exploitative nature of colonial rule. This was also the beginning of an alternative discourses on development in the colonies.

Anti-imperialism as Development

India was not an exception to this. To begin with the construction of India as a nation in the modern sense owes a lot to this particular anti-colonial movement that started in the second-half of the 19th century. It is an irony that this construction was done by taking a negative position both by the coloniser as well as the colonised. The former united it under one polity for the first time in its long history in order to facilitate proper exploitation, while the latter constructed the image of a united India in order to fight the former both in terms of strategies and tactics. Many a time it was so mechanical and point counter point in demagogy and polemics that it even belied the actual happenings in economy and society. But, history is a testimony to prove that in the long run the anti-imperialist struggle gained more popularity and larger support from the masses.

Finally, India along with the other former colonies attained freedom after the Second World War. It was expected that the new political and economic formations in the country would contribute in articulating positive construct of the country but, unfortunately, once again it continued to be a distant dream even today. The agony of partition and associated communal holocaust resulting into the formation of religious nationalism in the Indian subcontinent have contributed significantly in belying all such hopes. The partition of the country and the communal hatred and violence have become the most potent tools in the hands of the new rulers in both the countries to underplay the basic issues that are confronting the masses in both the countries and engage them in jingoistic nationalism. In fact, the construction of India and Pakistan has become the "other" to each other. India is projected that is "non-Pakistan" and Pakistan that is "non-India". This has been most successfully utilised by the rulers in both the countries to keep the political power in their hands.

Anti-Pakistan as Development

It was mentioned earlier that during the colonial days there were two important development paradigms or discourses prevalent in India. On the one hand the imperial power continued their exploitation in the name of development and the nationalists too raised the freedom struggle and liberation movements for ending exploitation, drain of wealth and proper development on the other. Today, the anti-imperialist construction of India has been replaced by anti-Pakistan construction in India. Similar things are taking place in Pakistan too. Pakistan is held responsible for most of the ills including regional tensions, insurgencies and also for the diversion of our meagre resources to non-developmental activities. The use of such a construction has become all the more popular in the age of globalisation. Otherwise, one fails to understand the "U" turn in India's foreign policy and diplomacy in recent years. It is well known that India had always been at the forefront of anti-imperialist struggle world-over. It was also the founder member of the non-alignment movement but, today it is most actively pursuing the imperialist agenda of globalisation.

Their persistent neglect of the ever-increasing social disparities and regional inequalities have forced majority of their population to get disenchanted with the functioning of our politico-economic system itself. These poor masses live in a state of perpetual despair and disillusionment. However, there are a tiny minority sporadically distributed in almost all parts of the country that have strongly resented this and they are posing a serious challenge to the basic concept of one nation and nationalism and pan-Indian model of development.

Anti-Centrism-cum-Separatism as Development

"Things fall apart the centre cannot hold" : these words had prognosticated the future of human history. This seems to be true in case of the Nation states in the 21st century. Today's Nation states are in serious crises. But, the most significant one is posed by the crises of the project of modernity and the Enlightenment philosophy itself.[3] India is also a witness to these challenges. The anti-imperialist construction of development that was popular during the colonial days has got transformed into anti-centre, separatist and autonomy movements in the country. These movements are more articulated in the peripheral areas of the country. The North-Eastern region of the country has a distinction of being at the forefront of such movements. At present there are more than two dozen armed rebellion and insurgent movements active in this part of the country. The most common thing among all these movements is that they think that both their development and identity is at stake within the fold of Pan-Indian nation and nationalism. Therefore, they believe that for development freedom is a must and this is possible only through national liberation movements.

National Integration as Development

To counter the threat from the forces of separatism the ruling classes in the country are trying their level best to accomplish the triple objectives of our planning, i.e. economic development, sovereignty and national integration. In the age of globalisation we are told that we need to achieve national integration within and integration of India in the world market for proper development. It is irony that India that had its origin in the historic struggle against the world imperialism in the 19th and the 20th centuries is today actively propagating the ideology of neo-imperialism. The forces of globalisation that are being unleashed in the form of the MTO and the WTO have opened the process of neo-colonialism world over and the people are its worst victims.

The Development Talisman

The concept "Development" in its contemporary meanings, associations and repercussions was introduced in the aftermath of the Second World War by the then President of United States of America, Henry S. Trumen in 1949 through his "Four-Point Programme". Thereafter, "development for peace" became the ruling ideology and the universal ethics of the "Brave New World". It hinged upon the central axial of higher introduction of technology in production for overtly greater control over nature and natural environment but covertly to acquire greater access into the lives of individuals and culture groups for ever-increasing manoeuvrability. It was considered necessary for attaining higher degree of freedom and improved standard of living (quality of life) for humankind. It was also projected as the only "legitimate" and "rational" path available for "human emancipation" from the bondage of poverty and similar other scourges. Imposition of "Pax Economica" or "Development for Peace" became the quintessential feature in the post-Trumen era world over and most often it was at the cost of "Pax Populi" or "Vernacular Autonomy". Some of the important consequences of such an approach were that the paradigm of "development" acquired hegemonic importance under the leadership of World Monopoly Capitalism and catastrophe for the paradigm of social distributive justice, regional balance, politics of cultural difference and sustainable development.

India, along with many other post-colonial countries in general and their backward areas inhabited mostly by numerous tribal cultural groups in particular were exposed to the new *mantra* of development. Subsequently, they were also administered the logic of "technology as the grammar of power and freedom". The Nehru-Elwin controversy clearly showed the urgency and impatience on the part of Nehru to modernise the tribal people through administering higher doses of technology for development. For Elwin loss of identity and freedom of the tribal people was the non-negotiable basic minimum for their meaningful survival. Since the independence of India the North-Eastern region has been experiencing the enactment of the saga "Development-Modernisation" strategies through planned actions on the part of the state and the central governments.

Scholars have tried to construct various models and epistemics to comprehend the process over these years. In the remaining parts of this chapter attempts have been made to critically evaluate the rationale behind the "Rational Development Paradigm" in the context of themes like :

Nationalist *versus* Cultural Development Paradigm

It is evident from the 1951 draft resolution of the Indian planning document that the Indian government will aspire to obtain the triple objectives of economic development, defence of India's sovereignty and national integration. Thus, programmes and plans those were in favour of the national integration were also considered viable for development. These were preferred over the social well-being and at the cost of undermining regional diversities in terms of history, culture and identities. The North-Eastern region of India with its innumerable cultural identities and nationalities have always resented such plans. The emergence of regional political parties and a large number of insurgent movements too indicate the underlying resentment of the people against such approaches of development. The following table shows the extent and nature of the insurgent movements in the region.

Table 4.1

Insurgent Groups in the North-Eastern Region of India[4]

State	Major Organisations	Others
Assam	ULFA	
	NDFB	
Nagaland	NSCN(IM)	
	NSCN(K)	
Manipur	UNLF	KYKL, KCP, KNA, KNF, ZRA
	PLA	
Tripura	ATTP	
	NLFT	
Arunachal		VLVA
		UPVA
		ULMA
Meghalaya		ALMA
		HVC
		HALC
		HNLC

It is, therefore, imperative to understand the feeling of the people of the region with human consideration and it will be fallacious to call the troubles in the region as a mere law and order problem or the handiwork of the foreign anti-Indian forces.

Development *versus* Sustainable Development

It is an irony of history that at the time of independence of India when most of the areas of the country were getting consolidated under one governance and polity of the new nation most of the areas and communities of the region were partitioned. And surprisingly, the history textbooks mentioned only about the partition of Bengal and Punjab. Conspicuous omission of the partition of Mizoland, Nagaland, Tripuriland, Maiteiland and Ahomland etc. speaks about the concern shown by the planners and the scholars of the country to this region and its people. They are also fighting their due recognition in the records of history.

In the name of development lackadaisical economic development mostly along the pattern initiated by the colonial powers continue to persist in the region. This region continues to be the major raw material procuring region and market for the finished goods without any proper planning and development. The ongoing process of development continues to elude the issues related to social development and sustainable development. At present most of the industries established in the region are posing big hazards to the social and physical environment in the region.

State *versus* Civil Society : Dialectics of Development

There are differences of opinion among the scholars about the nature of civil society in India. There are some who believe that civil society is essentially an European concept and it was closely associated with colonisation modernisation paradigm of the west. Therefore, for development in the real sense one will have to either deconstruct or negate the civil society oriented development paradigm. There are some others who believe that India too have its own variety of civil society. In case of the North-Eastern region the tribal social organisation and other apparatuses of the state are organs of civil society in the region. With the introduction of District Council Administration in the Sixth Schedule Areas of the region the traditional civil society has been strengthened in the region and all the developmental activities should centre around these traditional institutions.

Power *versus* Empowerment Paradigm

It has been the common experiences under modernity that the power of market is negatively related to the empowerment of the humankind. Estrangement and alienation are some of the necessary and logical outcome of technology induced modernisation and development. This is one of the hardest fact to digest for the tribal communities in the region. Tribals are known for their oral and customary regulation and norms of social conduct. The contractual relation that have been unleashed by the market forces have contributed not only in differentiating the so far less differntiated society but there are clear evidences of well developed classes in these communities. Power that had remained with the general will of the village council or the village elders in most of the communities in the region are today vulnerable to the interplay of market forces. This has not only eroded the tribal social ethics but, it has also disempowered them beyond redemption. The future is uncertain not because there are crises but because there is no alternative available at present.

NOTES

1. Kaviraj, S.: "The Imaginary Institution of India", *Subaltern Studies* VII (ed.); Chatterjee, P. and Pandey, G., Oxford University Press, New Delhi, p.1.
2. Edney, M.H.: *Mapping an Empire : The Geographical Construction of British India 1765-1843.* University of Chicago Press, Chicago, 1997.
3. Butola, B.S.: "Crises of Nationalist Historiography and the Nationalist Discourses in the North-Eastern Region of India", *Proceedings of the NEIHA Eighteenth Session,* pp. 267-85.
4. Hazarika, S.: *Strangers of the Mist,* Viking, New Delhi, 1996.

5

GLOBALIZATION VIS-A-VIS REGIONAL DEVELOPMENT: Challenges before the North-Eastern States

Asok Kumar Maiti

First of all, the era of 'globalisation' has begun with expansion of trade and foreign investment in countries of which our country is one which had signed the agreement and got included in World Trade Organisation. Whether globalisation is preceding largely for the growth and poverty-reduction in all countries or only for so-called dynamic and powerful countries at the expense of poorer nations including our own is indeed a matter of debate.

The second is, whether ideological substance of regional development policies for creating and for fortifying Indian Economy in order to ensure productive employment for the whole population through expansion as well as efficient use of natural and human resources for supply of goods and services to meet the genuine needs of the people of India is still valid and relevant in the era of globalisation.

Lastly, whether regional development aiming at national integration is at all compatible with the philosophy of globalisation and what are the challenges that India has to confront in the incoming millennium.

Globalization in Words and Deed

The gulf between promises and designs, precepts and practices so characteristic of the ruling political parties in the Nation-States is not alien to international bodies like United Nations (UN), International Monetary Fund (IMF), World Bank (IBRD) and World Trade Organisation (W.T.O.). UN bodies in their decade-long campaign (in 1990s) were promising milk and honey for all by 2000, namely "health for all" (eradication of leprosy, tuberculosis, malnutrition and what not)", "literacy for all", "shelter for all" and many other such things. But the promises never included 'employment for all able-bodied human beings' without which not even *Aladin* or *King of Ghosts* can provide anything to anybody. All these campaigns were in peak when the annual budget of UN (to which 185 states having 6 billion peoples contribute) was a meagre 4.6 billion dollars equivalent to 80 cents a year per human being compared with 134 dollar per person spent annually on arms and military.

Again, the most dominant economic campaign of 1990s was 'globalisation' when the world became almost unipolar following the disintegration of USSR and their reversion to capitalism along with the East European countries. The *description* of globalisation is the widening and deepening of international flows of trade, finance and information in a single integrated global market whereas the *prescription* for this was to liberalise national and global markets. The prescription cannot be administered at will on the sovereign states by force of arms as in 19th or early 20th century. Therefore the process should have to be more subtle, clever as well as riskless so that plundering of the resources of the weaker states is legitimised and sanctioned. For doing so, the governments of the states should be agreeable to changes necessary and therefore a well thought-out logic, namely "Economic Reforms" was formulated. These reforms are mainly liberalisation of national market and free entry of the multinationals, privatisation of economy, free competition among enterprises as well as countries, irrespective of their economic power. For these reforms to be undertaken, there should be flexible structure of administration and governance for which there should be the Structural Adjustment Programme (SAP). If all these go well in the less-developed and developing countries, the highly industrialised countries and the multinational and trans-national corporations incorporated in those countries can control all the economic, social and cultural activities of the poorer nations and the poor peoples of all the nations with impunity and conviction. Such is the design of globalisation.

Advocates of this economic phenomenon in the academic world presented their views with such an air of conviction and inevitability that even the majority of intellect-workers in our country seemed to believe them. Not since the heyday of *laissez faire* of the 19th century had economic theory elicited such wide-spread certainty.

The principles of global markets envisages that, the market for labour would be as free as the market for export or capital. Negotiation went on for instituting a free world market in foreign investment and services. In the last decade with trade liberalisation and free flow of foreign investment, the developing countries however experienced the widening of the already existing gaps among them. Meanwhile, in many industrialised including G-7 countries there was soaring unemployment not experienced since the great depression in 1930s and income-inequality increasing to levels not recorded since the last century. Though industrialised countries benefited in response to the new opportunities offered to them, they are not finding any solution to their own domestic economic problems especially unemployment. They are therefore desperately exploring newer outlets for investment of funds and putting pressure on the governments of less developed countries to create opportunities for unhindered movement of capital and goods globally.

For the world as a whole, the benefits of globalisation and liberalisation should exceed the cost. The estimated increase in global income between 1995 and 2001 was supposed to be 210 to 510 billion dollars (as a result Uruguay round of GATT) but this increase would only be concentrated in a group of countries at the cost of the poorer nations who are supposed to lose around 6 million dollars a year whereas the sub-Saharan Africa would lose 1.2 billion dollars.

The emerging scenario in the next millennium is very depressing in the sense that, in developing countries foreign exchange losses will translate into pressure on income, a diminishing ability to sustain imports and increased dependence on 'aid' at a time when 'aid' itself is under severe pressure. Revenue from trade would be decreased thereby inhibiting these governments to develop the economic and social infrastructure on which sustained reduction in human poverty depends.

Again, several studies have showed that growth did not help poverty-reduction when larger portions of increased income go out of the country in public expenditure such as repayment of foreign loan or for purchasing weapons.

Noam Chomsky in his *Profit over People* analysed this phenomenon as an attempt to bring the lives and livelihood of peoples under the hegemony of US and other multinational capital. He further showed that there is no liberalism in the process of liberalisation and no global element in the process of globalisation. There is marked protectionism in the industrialised countries which would bring in ruins to the less developed economies and not bring gains to poorer sections of people of the industrialised countries but to the multinational capital of those countries which would harvest the gains of international trade.

The recent controversy among the industrialised nations in World Trade Organisation over Multilateral Agreement of Investment (MAI) exposed the design of the multinationals which seek to ensure the rights of multinational corporations in all countries. Although there is yet to be a consensus among them, the negotiations are on to contemplate such a 'Charter of Rights'. If such an agreement is reached, no multinational corporation would be bound to pay any compensation if there is any damage done to lives and property of the workers or the people of the host country (mostly developing countries) in case there is any accident. In other words, Union Carbide could not be held responsible in any way for Bhopal tragedy if the said MAI is accepted.

Since the early 1970s the less developed countries have suffered a cumulative decline of 50 per cent in their terms of trade. For developing countries as a group, the cumulative terms-of-trade losses amounts to 290 billion US dollars between 1980 and 1991. Much of the catastrophic fall was due to decline in real commodity prices (in 1990 they were 45 per cent lower than in 1980 and 10 per cent lower than the lowest price during Great Depression in 1932). But poor prices were not confined to commodities alone. Developing countries' terms of trade for manufactured goods also fell by 35 per cent during 1970-1991.

Added to this was unfavourable terms in finance. With inferior credit ratings and the expectations of national currency depreciation, they paid interests that were in effect four times as high as those charged to rich countries during the 1980s. In part as a result of high interest rates, debt remains a millstone for many poor countries. Beyond the human cost, debt created economic obstacles. For LDCs debt repayments typically soak up about a fifth of export earnings seriously depleting their limited foreign exchange reserve and undermining their ability to engage in international trade on equitable terms. Moreover, poor countries are likely to lose because rules of game are biased against them. Developing countries with 75 per cent of world's population are supposed to get only a quarter of the income gains generated whereas most of the gains would go to a few powerful exporters in Asia and Latin America. The Uruguay round left intact most of the protections for industry and agriculture in industrialised countries while ignoring issues of vital concern notably the problem of debt and the management of primary commodities market in the poorer countries.

Under the 1994 agricultural agreement of the Uruguay round the developing countries had to liberalise imports of agricultural commodities which resulted in plight of small and marginal farmers and other agricultural workers in those countries. The problem is acutely illustrated by Philippines. Under the agreement Philippines had to liberalise imports of a wide range of agricultural commodities. For maize, tariffs and imports were halved over the next 8 years and minimum import quantities expanded. So depending on world price trends maize imported from US was 30 per cent cheaper than the domestic farm-gate prices. It would mean, around 1.2 million households who derived more than 3/4th of their income from maize sales would lose their livelihood. In the long run, "trade liberalisation will increase average income" need to be set against these human costs. This resembles Keynes' observation that 'in the long run we (or they?) are all dead'.

Such facts suggest that whatever may be the imagination of the advocates of free trade, it is conspicuously absent in the real world situation. The full extent of the unequal competition into which producers of Philippines are being forced is the process in the making for the poor producers of all other less developed and developing countries.

The State of Development : National and Regional

In case of India in spite of its planned economic development for 50 years it remained a country of stark contrast and disparities with a vast area remaining undeveloped or nominally developed. North-Eastern states and many parts of Eastern states (North Bihar, North Bengal etc.) belong to these underdeveloped regions.

With a population over 100 crore in the Indian societies, around 38 crore of Indians still cannot afford two square meals a day, 42 crore have no proper clothing, 30 crore are either homeless or live in precarious conditions and 55 crore are deprived of medical facilities even after 53 years of independence and in the beginning of the Third Millennium. More than 90 per cent of the population face the problem of declining water tables, quality problems and contamination of water. In 1994, rural poverty was 39 per cent and urban poverty was 30 per cent. There was steady improvement of income of the rural households from mid-70s to the end of 80s. Between 1977-78 and 1985-86 rural income poverty fell from 51 per cent to 39 per cent; by 1989-90 it had fallen to 34 per cent. Income poverty also fell in urban areas, from 40 per cent to 33 per cent between 1977-78 and 1989-90. During the period following economic reform after 1991, there was first a rise, then a fall in income poverty. In 1989-90 the incidence of income poverty in rural areas was 34 per cent; in 1992, 43 per cent; and in 1993-94, 39 per cent; in urban areas in these years it was 33 per cent, 34 per cent, and 30 per cent respectively. But these national aggregates mask wide variations among states. Four states managed to reduce income poverty to more than 50 per cent — Andhra Pradesh, Haryana, Kerala and Punjab. Other states were less successful as 50 per cent of India's rural income-poor now live in Bihar, M.P. and U.P.

How much of the reduction in poverty can be ascribed to economic growth? Growth was slower in 1950-75, averaging 3.6 per cent a year. Over the next 10 years, when income poverty fell the most, growth rose to 4 per cent a year, and in 1986-91 it averaged 6 per cent a year. But equating growth with poverty reduction is too simplistic. In the second-half of the 1980s, for example, despite rapid economic growth, income poverty fell little. Statistical analyses suggest that economic growth explains at best around 50 per cent of the reduction in income poverty.

Whether growth translates into human poverty reduction depends on social and political factors. Kerala, for example, ensured big reductions in income poverty, despite slow economic growth, through political activism and rapid, equitable expansion of opportunities.

Uneven progress in reducing human poverty (the denial of choices and opportunities for a tolerable life) is most marked in India. The indigenous people mostly tribals are poorer than other groups and most of them have been pushed to the marginal land. They also fare worse in non-income dimensions. Indigenous children receive much less education than non-indigenous children. Even when one of them earns enough education he feels discrimination in case of employment, settlement and social access. They also face challenges to maintain their own identity as values and customs cherished by them are distorted by the incoming population. Such deprivation sows seeds of dissatisfaction among masses and they live as 'foreigners' in their own land.

The growth we need in India must be expanding the opportunities and life choices of poor people, namely employment, productivity, wages of poor people as well as public expenditure for development of the poor. Human Development Report 1996 showed how a virtuous cycle of economic growth and human development takes over when the pattern of growth is labour intensive and employment generating and when there are rapid improvement of human skills and health. In fact this further showed that reducing poverty would be good for growth. Growth goes wrong because of the initial income-inequality. U.N. studies estimated that growth of 10 per cent reduced incidence of income poverty by 30 per cent where inequality is less (Gini ratio 0.25) and by only 10 per cent in less equal societies with the Gini ratio 0.50 as in India.

Whether growth is channelled to improve the income of the poor can be seen by comparing the growth of average per capita income with the growth of the incomes of the poorest 20 per cent. In case of Brazil and UK, GNP per capita grew by 3.1 per cent and 2.2 per cent whereas incomes of poorest 20 per cent increased by 0.80 per cent and 0.3 per cent respectively. No wonder that income poverty in these countries increased.

The cry for industrialisation by the political leaders, administration as well as a major section of intelligentsia assuming that the economy would be set into growth path should indeed be judged in the light of our past experiences. To quote Human Development Report 1997, "Industrialisation has brought fewer benefits for the poor......Brazil, India and Mexico have industrialised without substantially reducing poverty — mainly because they distorted prices, interest rates and exchange rates to favour capital intensive investment". Reinforcing this tendency were labour laws and policies favouring a few fortunate workers in the organised sector and sowing the seeds of division and discord among the reserve army of labour.

So even if so called globalisation promotes growth in our country it is likely that income poverty would tend to rise. This observation should not be misconstrued as an anti-growth argument but as an advocacy for the change in the socio-economic structure of the society so that distribution of gains becomes equitable even within our system of development.

The questions and issues of regional development should also be approached from similar view point, namely whether the growth of Indian Economy ensures the growth of different regions within it and the states within the regions. If so, one can find some solution to the problems of underdevelopment.

As against the goals of liberalisation, policies conceived in our planned economic development should be reviewed. The fact remained that peoples' aspiration for improvement of the quality of life in the wake of freedom was self-sustaining and self-reliant economic development through a thorough overhaul of our socio-economic structure. It was also realised that there was acute intra- and inter-regional differences within our country. There was different kinds of livelihood at different regions among different ethnic groups used to different modes of living beginning from pastoral-nomadic mode to capitalist mode. There was social, economic and technological dualism in both primary and secondary sectors of production. The service sector was also not that developed. There was acute shortage in production of food and the country had no strong industrial base. Taking all these into consideration, emphasis was first put on agriculture and then on basic industries gradually making way for walking on both legs (industry as well as agriculture). In order to bring about national integration (in fact nation-building) what was urgently needed was emphasis on development of the people in different regions so that a kind of Indianness could be cultivated among even the most backward community of people. Therefore regional development was indispensable part of our national planning for development.

Regional development having three major aims (productive, social and biological) was an attempt to secure best conditions and possibilities for an all-round development for everybody; minimise and ultimately eliminate inter-regional and intra-regional differences in quality of life and make the best possible use of the natural resources and human values of the region to secure the production and social aims. These aims are comprehensive in nature and not restricted to economic (productive) aspects alone. They emphasise on distributive justice so that the differences in levels of living could be eliminated creating conditions for all-round development of all people of the regions. The philosophical foundation of such policy should therefore be based on co-operation rather than on competition whereas the multinational's mandate for globalisation, liberalisation and structural adjustment is the philosophical outcome of the "survival of the fittest".

It should be remembered that social structure of the developing societies whether conceived in the national or regional levels is inhibitive of progress. The benefits of increased development in economic and social activities in these areas go to those who need them least. But investments to raise the level of living of the people should percolate downwards, upwards, sideways so that everybody gets benefit. This leads to greater participation of all people in productive activities. Nobody progresses unless all progress and co-operation and mutual support should orient the development policies. Surplus productions would naturally get recycled for mutual benefit or in an inter-regional system gets invested in other regions to bring about inter-regional equity in development.

The *description* of our kind of development should therefore be the processes through which a society acquires greater porosity within its own body politic and enables its members to gain greater control over themselves and their environment. For this, the primary consideration should be transforming the social structures and institutions especially restructuring production, changes in social structure, cultural change and changes in political and legal structure. Then only an economy can be geared to ensure productive employment for the whole population. The provision of health, education and similar other facilities is only a secondary aspect of social development which may be necessary but neither sufficient nor possible except making any headway in transforming social structure making our permeable society to a porous one.

The aims of regional development mentioned above need a comprehensive social development policy suitable for a developing country like India. But regional development encompassing not only productivity and income but also structural change in class and interest group relations so that broad masses of working people are able to participate and share in productivity leading to increased welfare in gross as well as 'net' terms should be the *prescription* of development. For this, policy of increasing growth automatically trickling down below canvassed till now, should be rejected.

The inadequacy of prevalent theories and practices of regional development (mostly disaggregated versions of western macro-economic growth models) is that, development is conceived merely in terms of steady growth of production and income whereas social class interests and group relations which form the basis of distribution of the gains of development are assumed to change with increase in productivity. Human beings are treated not as goal but as factor of production and recipients of particular marginal investment through public expenditure in social welfare programmes such as health, education, housing, social security and so on. Social policies therefore reduce to operational allocation of various residual resources derived from national system for redistribution and for partially covering the accumulated deficit in certain social welfare services.

The government as well as the academia by and large accepts globalisation as inevitable in the plea of TINA (There Is No Alternative). If that is so, one is to accept that policies for national or regional development are irrelevant in the wake of globalisation. In case of international policy options the questions of relevance of states is also dubious. At one level the state is being resisted by ethnic and other groups pressing for greater autonomy and "self-determination". At other level, they are being bypassed by the MNCs who give a damn to local jurisdiction. *States therefore become too big for the small things and too small for the big.* This has to be so as total corporate sales of top five corporations is 871.4 billion US dollars whereas the GDP of South Asia as a whole is 451.3 billion US dollars (UNDP report 1997). These big things pose challenges for international governance as the mechanism for managing the system is inadequate threatening to disturb stability by persistently impoverishing much of the world. The playing fields of globalisation slopes against the peoples and countries.

All kinds of ethnic, religious and secessionist conflicts are being deliberately cultivated by vested interests within the states or nations directly or indirectly aided and abetted by foreign MNCs. Peoples' aspirations for self-determination and self-reliance are being wrongly utilised by parochial and fundamentalist forces of different hues. In such cases extremely opposite group interests are performing the same task of undermining national sovereignty of the weaker states or nations. Today's globalisation sought by GATT or IMF or for that matter MNCs is meant to wipe away national borders and wipe out national policies for 'development', be it national or in regional planes. One can have a bird's eyeview of the underdevelopment situation inter-regionally within our own country which would indicate relative deprivation and underprivileged situation of the North-Eastern region. The data themselves are a strong argument for the need for regional development of North-Eastern states aiming at national integration.

State	Basic socio-economic indications of development				
	NDP per capita at current prices (1995-96)	Infant mortality rate (%) (1990-92)	Life expectancy (1988-91)	Literacy rate (1991)	Employment rate (1991)
Punjab	15504	5.7	65.46	58.51	30.87
Haryana	13770	7.1	62.74	55.85	N.A.
Andhra Pradesh	8615	7.1	60.64	44.49	45.05
Kerala	8324	1.7	70.76	89.79	31.43
Tamil Nadu	9868	5.8	60.83	62.66	43.31
West Bengal	7851	6.6	59.75	57.70	32.19
North-Eastern States					
Assam	6192	7.6	55.47	52.90	46.24
Manipur	7277	2.4	N.A.	59.89	42.18
Mizoram	7743	N.A.	N.A.	82.27	48.19
Nagaland	6638	1.0	N.A.	61.65	42.68
Meghalaya	6826	5.8	N.A.	49.10	42.67
Arunachal Pradesh	10933	6.4	N.A.	41.59	46.24
Tripura	4376	5.4	N.A.	60.44	31.14
India	N.A.	8.0	58.58	52.19	37.48

Source : Economic & Political Weekly, May 1994; Government of India, Indian Economic Survey 1997-98.

It is clearly revealed from the above data that :

(i) comparing with other major states in India, the NDP per capita is much lower in all the North-Eastern states except in Arunachal

Pradesh.

(ii) the incidence of infant mortality is highest in Orissa (12%), followed by M.P. (11.1%), U.P. (9.8%), Rajasthan (8.4%) and Assam (7.6%). Except Nagaland where the infant mortality rate is very low (1%), in all other states in the North-Eastern region the rate is significantly high.

(iii) life expectancy is lowest in Rajasthan (44.7), followed by U.P. (52.03) and Assam (55.47) which are even lower than the Indian average (58.58).

(iv) it has been observed that except in Arunachal Pradesh all the states in the N.E. regions achieved success in literacy rates.

(v) from the employment point of view, the states in the N.E. regions have comparatively better employment rate than in other Indian states. One need not be happy with this because per capita NDP is much lower than in other Indian states. This phenomenon clearly indicates that the income-generating activities are such that labour is paid poorly which is a clear sign of underdevelopment. Hence the people of N.E. states continue to live a very low standard of living.

The Challenges Ahead

Such being the situation of our economy in national and regional plans the incoming millennium brings forward some specific challenges.

The challenges before the people of our country in the coming millennium are manifold and varied. The first and foremost of the challenges is to maintain the limited economic sovereignty and further it as one nation and people by opting for independent and self-reliant development (not Nehruvian but truly independent model).

Short-sighted policies generally pursued by the government that be in the centre with an eye to vote-bank and increasingly relying for electoral expenses on business houses including the multinationals be resisted by the working class, peasantry and the intelligentsia and there should be workers' and peasants' own organisations to carry forward the task of social change.

To cope with the present-day development of Science and Technology, mutual co-operation with other countries on sovereign basis should be established and emphasis should be given on the relationships with the neighbouring countries (China, Sri Lanka, Pakistan, Bangladesh, Nepal, Bhutan — East Asian countries and countries with similar interests).

For reduction of income poverty, growth is necessary (though not sufficient as discussed above) but the growth should be oriented towards the poor depending on the real situation in our country. The major consideration of such growth should be to integrate the eradication of poverty and regional under-development in sectoral and national development strategies. The priorities should be made clear for our country where the majority of the populations earn their living from agricultural activities in small-farms.

So raising productivity in small-scale agricultural sector, emphasising on labour-intensive industrialisation for expanding employment opportunities, acceleration of the expansion of human capabilities and skill (capabilities by socio-economic overhaul and skill by appropriate educational policy for training), establishing a pro-poor economic policy framework should be the foci of our activities. Land reforms aiming as gradual socialisation of land, restoring of the community ownership of land on voluntary basis, employment-led urban development by expanding service sector should form the cornerstone of our development policies. The mega projects like large dams, large plants which displace poor people from their habitats and throw them out of employment should be stopped and appropriate policies for eco-friendly and pro-people development be pursued.

In lieu of Conclusion

In view of the above discussion about the incompatibility of globalisation and regional as well as national development, it is difficult to draw any conclusion by way of saying simple 'no', or 'yes' to market economics, globalisation etc. as such conclusion would be too simplistic.

Nearly for more than half a century between 1880 and 1945 monopoly capitalism was established. The capitalist single thought at that period was 'monopolistic nationalistic liberalism'. According to Samir Amin, Liberalism signifies predominant role of markets (oligopolistic markets, to be sure) in a self-regulating economy within structure of appropriate public policies and bourgeois democratic political practice. Nationalism was a regulating fact within this liberal model able to legitimise public policies underlying competition within the global system. Those policies hinged on local hegemonic coalitions (alliance of middle class-aristocrat strata) that backed the dominant power of capitalist monopolies. Likewise, these alliances were reinforced through colonial privileges. Electoral democracy based on these alliances allowed flexible adjustment of the terms for their maintenance. So the state was needed for management of hegemonic coalition by organising and regulating markets appropriately and for directing its international competitive strategy. Its active intervention in this sense was considered as legitimate and necessary. This so-called national liberal single thought fell into crisis in 1914 as economic competition turned to World War including its fascist deviations. Fascism abandoned the politically democratic aspect of the system but renounced neither nationalism nor the internal social compromises that bolstered the power of monopolies.

Fascist thought remained therefore a component, though a sick one of the ruling single thought of this long phase in the history of capitalism. It took Second World War which upset the balance of social forces in favour of working class. Amin characterised the single thought of the 1945-1980 as perod as 'social and national' operating within the framework of controlled globalisation — simplistically called 'Keynesian'. It did not make any radical break with liberalism but made some rearrangements (collective bargaining, social insurance, wage increases linking with productivity etc.). So the permanently imperialist dimension of the capitalist political economy remained in force. The globalisation thesis proclaimed so arrongantly by its current ideologues is nothing but a new way in which the inherently imperialist nature of the system asserts itself. So for all practical purposes globalisation is the euphemism for the recently unuttered word 'imperialism' and the so called free market forces indicate neo-colonialist plunder of the weaker nations and their peoples. In this sense regional and national development would be shelved for all practical purposes in the current era of globalisation.

At this point the most pessimistic of vision, capitalism constitutes the bounds of possible evolution, is the end of history as Francis Fukuyama or 'end of civilisation' as Nirod C. Choudhury ingenuously claimed. This evolution yields the apocalyptic vision of *pure war* an inexorable advance towards the extinction of human race.

As opposed to this there is an alternative to this kind of future which can be shaped by the working people and the reserve army of unemployed which are now no longer separated geographically and politically but are both present in metropolitan and peripheral countries alike. It therefore creates conditions for renewed struggle confronting economic alienation and rebel against global polarisation and destruction of national environment aiming at development for all the people of all nations including the development at regional and sub-regional planes. Such are the new requirements of theories and practices in the new millennium.

I firmly believe that patriotic intellectual workers in spite of their ideological and other differences would join hands and heads to face the recent challenges in both academic and administrative planes.

REFERENCES

Amin, Samir, 1996, *Capitalism in the Age of Globalisation,* Zed Press, London, 1996.

Amin, Samir, 1999, *Spectres of Capitalism,* Rainbow Publications Limited, Delhi, 1999.

Chenay, H.B., 1961, Comparative Advantage and Development Policy, *American Economic Review,* Vol. 51, March 1961.

Chomski, Noam, 1999, *Profit over People,* Madhyan, Delhi, 1999.

Kluiten Brouwer, J.B.W., 1973, "On the Concept of Process of Marginalisation", in *Occasional Paper No. 37,* The Hague, ISS, 1973.

Misra, R.P., D.V. Urs and U.K. Natraj (ed.), 1978, *Regional Planning and National Development,* Vikas, Delhi, 1978.

Misra, R.P., *et al.,* 1974, *Regional Development Planning in India — A New Stratgey* Vikas, Delhi, 1974.

UNDP, 1996, *Human Development Report-1996,* OUP, 1996

UNDP, 1997, *Human Development Report-1997,* OUP, 1997.

6

GLOBALIZATION AND NORTH-EAST INDIA : Opportunities and Challenges for the Twenty-first Century

J. B. Ganguly

Structural Changes during the Colonial and Post-Independence Periods

The Nineteenth century was the century of colonial domination over NEI. Along with the colonial rulers came the Christian Missionaries who carried out their mission of converting the local people, particularly of the tribal areas, to Christian religion and of promoting social development by opening educational institutions, developing local dialect into written languages, establishing health care units, centres for imparting training in simple technical trades, etc. Functioning of the colonial administrative structure and the different organs of Government directly or indirectly established by the colonial power and that of the Christian missionaries promoted the process of modernization-cum-westernization in NEI. All these changes were not peaceful in all cases. There were violent uprisings of the indigenous communities who valiantly tried to resist the penetration of the British authority and even the Christian missionaries into their respective areas. But ultimately the colonial power prevailed being in possession of superior military might in terms of weaponry, command structure, resources and in knowledge.

The colonial rule came to an end in 1947 and India emerged as post-colonial state of the Union of India as a federal republic which included the different parts of NEI. The second half of the twentieth century has been distinguished by the move of institutionalization of the indigenous democratic structure at the local level and the creation of the constitutionally defined states as the federating units of the Union of India. These changes have opened up the space of people's participation in the political and economic decision-making processes above the village level. These changes have not, however, been without opposition at the sub-regional and regional level. Such dissents are yet to be fully resolved even as the twentieth century had come to an end.

The second half of the twentieth century has also been the era of state-sponsored planned process of economic and social development.

North-East India's Encounter with Globalization

The twenty-first century will be the century of NEI's involvement in the process of globalization of its economy and other spheres of life. The process would throw up a great challenge before the people of NEI who have to take advantage of new opportunities without compromising their core values.

Wide gamut of tremendous technological advances particularly in information technology, formidable rise of transnational corporations, growing involvenment of international economic agencies under the aegis of the UN in influencing the policies of member-nations, rise in the propotion of contribution of international trade to the growth rate of GNP of all nations, etc. have been promoting the spirit of globalisation and the emergence of the global economy into which the economies of countries all over the world including India have been getting willy nilly integrated. The main objective of the process of globalization is to achieve competitive efficiency for optimization of resource use at the global level. This will depend on withdrawal of trade barriers or at least lowering of the levels of tariff walls and loosening of restrictions on flow of resources across national frontiers.

The process of globalization is not the panacea for the developing countries to quicken the pace of achieving growth and development for eradication of poverty. The process of globalization, as pointed out by the UNDP, has not ensured the distribution of benefits evenly amongst nations and within nations. It has been particularly violating the principle of equity. The process of globalization does not only affect economic performances of people but also their social, political and cultural institutions and traditions (Shroff 1999: 2848).

The global perspective of oraganizing activities in different spheres of life is not an unknown phenomenon in NEI. Having access to the phenomenal development of information technology the people of the North-East are already aware of the global dimension of various developments and issues that affect their social, cultural, economic and political life-styles and activities.

The concept of globalization forms an essential element of the country's on-going economic reforms programme which entails the processes of privatization, liberalization and letting the competitive market economy to operate freely. Carrying out of such structural reforms in NEI will greatly upset the existing order of its socio-economic and political management system. In the post-Independence period, that is the second half of the twentieth century, the process of state-sponsored and state-directed planned social and economic development within the framework of positive discrimination in favour of the people has been in progress in NEI. An important aspect to this process relates to the enjoyment of the north-eastern states of preferential treatment in the matter of devolution of financial resources from the Centre for meeting their plan and non-plan expenditures.

The scheduled caste and scheduled tribe populations constitute 6.85 per cent and 25.8 per cent of the region's population respectively. The state-wise disaggregated figures are as follows: Scheduled tribe population in Arunachal Pradesh 63.60 per cent Assam 12.82 per cent, Manipur 34.42 per cent, Meghalaya 85.53 per cent, Mizoram 94.75 per cent, Nagaland 87.70 per cent and Tripura 31per cent (NEC 1994) for these categories of people there are constutionally provided reservation of jobs in the government services and public sector enterprises and institutions. Similarly places in educational institutions both general and technical are reserved for them. Membership of elected bodies at all levels starting from the local to state and central levels are also reserved for them in proportion to the sizes of their respective populations. Of course such categories of population in other parts of the country also enjoy the privilege of positive discrimination in their favour. Even then, such constitutional safeguards compromise the principle of free competition for jobs, seats in institutions, etc. And this feature constitutes an important component of the socio-economic and political management system that has evolved in the region.

Another element of negation of liberalism in economic institutional management system relates to the fact that there does not exist free markets for productive resources, such as land, land-based and other indigenous resources. Freedom of enterprise for the non-tribals in the tribal-majority states and tribal areas of other north-eastern states is also largely non-existent. Under the Inner Line Regulation, freedom of entry of citizens from other parts of the country and abroad is also restricted.

Formulation and incorporation of all these restrictive and positive discriminatory provisions in our Constitution was necessary because at the given low level of social and economic development of the people of this region and their cultural milieu of egalitarianism the so-called market competition would be disastrous and highly unfair. It was also required to be ensured that the tribal people's rights in land and forests should be respected and that the people should develop along the lines of their own genius. Nehru also cautioned against introducing too many outsiders into tribal territory and against over-administering these areas. He further implored that development work in these areas should be implemented 'through, and not in rivalry to, their own social and cultural institutions.' The people were also not to be overwhelmed by a multiplicity of schemes (Ganguly, 1992: 143).

Shortcomings of Centrally Sponsored Planning Regime

The centrally sponsored planning regime that has been extended to this region has the objective of building a socialistic pattern of society in the country as envisaged by Nehru. This is backed by the concept of mixed economy in which the public sector and the private sector of productive activities co-exist and the respective shares of each sector are defined and earmarked by the government. The on-going model of economic management entails an host of government controls, regulations, protections, subsidization of productive activities, etc. In such an environment those who wield state power, namely the politicians and bureaucrats can usurp many kinds of personal benefits and opportunities of acquring wealth, influence and power even by resorting to corrupt practices.

Over the years there have been deviations from Nehru's pronounced policy of development for this region. An opinion poll conducted by the North-East Girl Students' Coordination Committee, extracts from which were published in the press in January 2000, reveals that 'corruption and gross misuse of public funds' are the primary reasons for the backwardness of the North-East (*The Statesman,* Calcutta, 31 January, 2000). The system is not only giving rise to social, political and economic inequalities but it is also suppressing individual enterprise and initiative and curbing the role of the community in guiding social responses to changes affecting their lives. The Government's approach amounts to almost spoon-feeding the people to achieve progress as envisaged by the former.

P.A. Sangma, the then Chief Minister of Meghalaya, in his inaugural speech at the seminar on 'Jawaharlal Nehru and the Disadvantaged' held at Shillong on 25 and 26 September, 1989 highlighted the adverse effects of the Government of India's policy of quickening the pace of development through conciliation and short term economic relief in order to contain tribal insurgencies in North-East India. Admitting that in the initial phase Government's policy yielded rich dividends, he stated, "but it is now time to have a close reappraisal of them in the light of experience gathered" (1992:7). He laments that the Government's actions have "generated a tendency towards causing dependence on the Government in so far as economic wherewithal is concerned. The tribals have lost to an extent the spirit of self-dependence, so characteristic of tribal society and so essential for building up a sound base for progress that has been badly impaired" (p. 8).

Harmful Impacts of Globalization

Under the economic reforms programme started in 1991 the process of globalization of the economy has not been an unmixed blessing. While exports of the country have been growing steadily, faster growth of imports of consumer goods produced by multi-national corporations has been severely affecting Indian industries particularly in the small scale sector. Thousands of these units are either dying or becoming sick, resulting in the rise in unemployment level. If this is the condition of the long established industrial units in other parts of India, growth of small and household industries will be further stunted if the economy of the region is fully opened up. Moreover, entry of MNCs will lead to rapid exhaustion of the natural resources which form, as it were, the life support system of the people. Another lurking danger relates to loss of the region's rich stock of bio-diversity. One of the banes of globalization has been the phenomenon of bio-piracy. North-East India will have to remain ever vigilant against the MNC's attempts at obtaining patents for many indigenous plants, herbs and extractions that people have been traditionally using.

'Globalization', according to the joint report by the World Health Organization and the Voluntary Health Association of India, 'has hit women badly'. The report points out: "The process of Globalization has affected the poor badly especially women in terms of increase in trafficking of women and prostitution, greater spread of female foeticides and female infanticides, dowry demands, harassment and dowry death" (Quoted in *The Hindu,* Chennai, 8 July, 2000). Though the women of the North-East are set free from some of these evils, they are more susceptible to suffering on account of globalization, what Vandana Shiva, environmentalist has termed 'assault on hearth.' For "the agro-industry is the dominant sector in India's globalization programme, the well-known examples of multinationals in this sector being Cargill and Pepsi. This is the sector where an overwhelming majority of Indian women are active in food production and food processing.... So with globalization..... women's activities and their resources (are) moving out of the kitchen and hearth and into the hands of multinational corporations" (*The Statesman*, Calcutta, 1996). In such conditions women of the North-East would have to resist such possibilities of losing control over their resources and sources of livelihood.

"Greater connectedness also means," says Shroff, "faster transmission of ideas and skills, good and bad". One fallout of this development is the phenomenon of cultural invasion from abroad' which is 'a threat to the survival of national traditions and values' (1999 : 2848). For the people of the North-East preservation of their ethnic identity is an important concern. In the increasingly globalized world neither India as a country nor North-East India as one of its regions can remain indifferent to this. It is also true that when one opens the windows one gets fresh air as well as insects and mosquitoes. The answer is not to shut the window, but may be to put a screen or install an insect repellant. In other words, we must improve our understanding of the national and internal policies to tackle the possible adverse impact of globalization.

Suggested New Development Paradigm

In the context of the process of globalization the people of the North-East need to be empowered to decide and take initiative in improving their conditions by their own enterprise and hard work in accordance with their own perception of development in an equitable manner. There should be a paradigm shift in the ongoing model of centrally dominated programme of development with centrally provided resources. People of the region must have the liberty to decide what would be the appropriate technology for their productive enterprises and at what pace they would take advantage of the technological changes for improvement of their social, cultural and economic conditions. They should also be able to control uses of their natural resources so that they can maintain a sustainable growth of their economy while preserving their rich biodiversity.

The new paradigm of development will entail devolution of power to the grassroots level for formulating and executing programmes of development with locally mobilized resources and supplemented by resources provided by the Centre. But the proportion of the former must be greater than the latter in sharp contrast with the existing ratio.

The civil society must play a vital role in ensuring effective participation of the people at the grassroots level in such a planning regime. The civil society has traditionally been the people's association for organizing their productive, distributive, judicial, cultural and ritualistic (or religious) activities. The process of incorporation of the tribal settlements into the modern state structure began during the colonial period but in much diluted form. The colonial administrative structure did not penetrate deeply into these areas. Whenever the colonial authority sought to interfere into their traditional customs and values it encountered resistance from the civil society. In the post-Independence period the process of transition from the tribal polity to that of the modern state structure culminated as full-fledged constitutionally defined units of the post-colonial Indian Union, a federation of states. But the civil society continued to play its part in civic, economic and political life of the people although the space of its operation got narrowed down. This trend has to be somewhat reversed and its role expanded in the globalized political, economic, social and cultural order.

REFERENCES

Ganguly, J.B. (1992), Nehru and the Evolution of the Policies and Programmes of Development of Tribal Areas in the North-East, published in *Jawaharlal Nehru and Disadvantaged,* Tripathi and Datta Ray, Shillong 1992, pp. 136-160.

North Eastern Council (1994), *NER at a Glance,* Shillong.

The Hindu, Chennai (2000), Globalization has hit Women Badly, 8-7-2000.

Sangma, P.A. (1992), "Teach them to catch Fish," published in *Jawaharlal Nehru and Disadvantaged,* Tripathi and Datta-Ray, Shillong.

Shroff, Manu (1999), Globalization : A Stock-Taking, *Economic and Political Weekly,* Mumbai, October 2-8, pp. 2845-49.

Shiva, Vandana (1996), Globalization: "Assault on Hearth," In an interview with Sumana Ramanan, Published in *The Statesman,* Calcutta, 13 February, 1996.

Tripathi, C.D. and Datta-Ray, B. (1992), *Jawaharlal Nehru and the Disadvantaged,* Department of Parliamentary Affairs, Government of Meghalaya and North East India Council for Social Science Research, Shillong.

7

CIVIL SOCIETY UNDER GLOBALISATION : A Case Study on "Assam Rural Infrastructure and Agricultural Services Project"

Asok Kumar Ray

In the European tradition the concept of Civil Society is traceable in the classical philosophy of Aristotle who gave the concept of 'Polis' to mean that society which dominates and controls all others. 'Polis' made no distinction between state and civil society. The term *'Societas Civilis'* appeared also in Cicero's thought in the early middle age with a view to upholding the autonomy of the temporal authority over the ecclesiastical authority. The distinction between state and civil society started to be felt more prominently during the mid-18th to mid-19th century in Britain, France and German states. Pluralisation of the concept of *'societas civilis'* thus emerged, had passed precisely through four overlapping spatio temporal phases.

In the first phase an attempt was made to simultaneously justify a specifically modern form of civil society — a sovereign, centralised, constitutional state standing over its subjects as a *'Societas civilis-cum-imperio imperium'* and to emphasise the strategic importance of guarding against its authoritarian potential by fostering the growth of independent states within civil society. The internal rupturing of the classical concept of civil society was noticed first in England and France. The opposition of *'societe naturale'* (the sphere of economic relation) to *'societe politique'* (the sphere of political relation) became a noticeable theme in physiocratic doctrine.

In the second phase a theme was crystallized that independent societies of a civil society could legitimately exist and defend against the state. This theme appeared once again in England and France in the background of the American and the French revolution controversy.

The third phase was a reversal to the second phase. This was found in the early Utilitarians (Bentham, Sismondi). The predominant adherence to this theme was found in the German thought whereby the necessity of regulation, restriction and integration of civil by means of politico-legal and administrative control was felt. This was implied in *'burgerliche gesselschaft'*. The fourth phase was marked by resurgence of autonomy of civil society against the regulatory state.[1]

It is worthwhile to mention here that by this time, (late 18th century to early 19th century) civil society assumed a dual meaning — the entrepreneurial guilds and the non-entrepreneurial social groups. This dualism between economic and normative civil society invariably brought forward an interesting hiatus. While on the one hand, the *laissez faire* doctrine rested on essential differentiation and separability of civil society and the state, and confined the state function to 'hindering the hindrances of good life' (i.e. unbridled economic pursuits), the non-entrepreneurial social groups, on the other hand, raised a debate on the autonomy of the latter and on limiting state action because their non-economic pursuits (scientific, literary, artistic, religious, cultural etc.) stood at odds with the accumulation of arbitrary state power which was meant to protect the corporate privileges of the entrepreneurial class.[2] It is from this point that the pluralist movement took a major turn.

In England John Locke was a landmark in the epistemology of civil society. His concept of civil society appeared in the context of the Glorious Revolution in England. This revolution gave him an occasion to provide an alternative to despotic government. Locke urged upon a self-government which stood for the sovereignty of the individual. His advocacy of individual right was so much so that he went to the extent of saying that an individual owed nothing to the state while the only and the chief function of the state was to protect private property of the individual. Locke viewed individual 'as pure abstraction, combining with the others to make the state, but himself wholly apart from the state'. In his Civil Government, Locke ignored all other forms of associations and their corporate sentiments including voluntary groups, trade unions, community organisations and churches.[3] His focus on Civil Governance provided an ideal institutional background to the budding capitalism in Europe.

George Hegel gave a more articulate view of civil society. To him, civil society stands for the realm of economic interest — labour, private property and class distinction. In other words, civil society refers to the material condition of life. At the same time, Hegel also recognised the realm of political society (state). He however launched the view that concrete freedom would lie in identifying the civil society to the state.

A culmination of this thought may be found in his concept of 'Ideal State'.[4] Hegel had so much similarity of thought with Locke. Both found civil society as providing a ground to the capitalist order. But there was dissimilarity as well. While Locke gave a subjective interpretation of civil society and a negative concept of law, freedom and universality, Hegel tended to argue for coexistence of subjective and universal within the civil society. Unlike Locke, Hegel made individuals obliged to abide by the decisions of the court. "Through the administration of justice, to Hegel, the unity of the individual and the universal would be achieved".[5]

The Hegelian logic behind combining the individual with the universal in the civil society rested on his strong advocacy for private property and class distinction. He intended to create that social condition in which private property and class distinction could be perpetuated. Thus when Hegel talked about duties and obligations of individuals, he pointed virtually at system maintenance of the propertiated class. Hence he brought in the concept of 'surveillance of public authority'[6] as a regulatory mechanism from above.

The semantic transformation of the concept of *'societas civilis'* is found to be intertwined to the transitional economic reality of early capitalism, commodity production and exchange. Thus Marx, unlike Hegel, gave to civil society a specific meaning. On the point of civil society, Marx differed from Hegel on two important counts — namely, combining the individual with the universal in civil society[7] and identifying the state to the civil society. Marx and Engels wrote:

> "Civil society comprises the entire material interaction among individuals at a particular evolutionary stage of productive forces. It comprises the entire commercial and industrial life of a state and hence transcends the state and the nation even though that life, on the other hand, manifested in foreign affairs as nationality and organised within a state. The term civil society emerged in the 18th century when property relations had already evolved from the community of antiquity and medieval times. Civil society as such develops within the bourgeoisie."[8]

Hence, individual-universal indentification, to Marx and Engels, is a myth as universal stands for the capitalist universe which rests on irreconcilable forces of contradiction between capital and labour.

In the epistemology of civil society Anthonio Gramsci was a break.

He intended to establish a normative and ethical basis of civil society and its role and potentiality in socio-economic life. He believed in inter-penetration of political society and economic society and recognised the autonomy of civil society in having a distinct sphere of operation and development. At the same time Gramsci brought in the concept of "Hegemony" to describe the complex and often hidden ways in which class domination seeps into social institutions, becoming particularly pervasive in advanced capitalist societies. "The bourgeois hegemony is a state of affairs in which the ideology of the doninant class becomes the acceptable common sense of the society, legitimizing the overwhelming power of the market and those who control its key institutions. Class rule extends beyond economy to the spheres of politics and culture. Schools, religious congregations, unions, hospitals, farmers' associations, community groups — in short — the civil society are, in Gramscian terms, all profoundly influenced by the logic of the 'natural order' of capitalism. Civil society is the location where the state operates to enforce invisible, intangible and subtle forms of power. The civil society disciplines the mind and the psyche through the institutions."[9] The implication of Gramscian civil society has been focused by Ajit Roy in the following manner :

> "The expansive structure of modern state which included the state institution as well as organisation of civil society resemble the trenches (in the fortification of a country's war front) in the shape of potential politics and serve as secure defence system in a war of position. In simpler terms, its essence is: because of expansion of civil society, the role of direct revolutionary uprising has become relatively reduced. In other words, without sufficiently reducing the ethical-ideological influence of the ruling class by waging war of position within various institutions of civil society, it will not be possible either to prepare for a revolutionary uprising or to ensure the final victory of a successful uprising.[10] In a more or less similar tone, Burnbawm stated that presence of strong civil society acts as a deterrent against political mobilisation that opposes the state.[11]

II. GLOBALISATION AND CIVIL SOCIETY

The Gramscian explanation of the ethico-normative bases of civil society has much resemblance to the practice on the part of the West. With the collapse of state socialism, the West started to rethink and reconsider the concept of civil society. This happened in East Europe and in the United

States. The ideological shift caused by the New Economic Policy and the Structural Adjustment Policy is marked by the return of the 19th century *laissez faire* values and culture to designate civil society once again a private sphere of capitalism. Thus when today the multinational corporations and the World Bank recognise the existence of civil society by passing the deep conceptual debate about that civil society that develops within the bourgeoisie, they have an axe to grind. Such civil societies are differently termed as non-governmental organisations, non-profit organisations or voluntary organisations. The non-political and non-profit features of such civil societies are apparently stressed upon. In recent times two other features have been added. One, these civil societies are highly regulated by the state laws and two, high professional values displacing altruism. This is found in the context of globalization. This development has taken place not only in the US where "contrary to the charitable nature of non profit organizations in the mid-19th century, high professionalism, managerial skill and techniques have been incorporated into the non-profit organization",[12] but also in the other countries with whom the multinational corporations, IMF and the World Bank collaborate through Foreign Direct Investment.

The increasing professionalisation and institutionalisation of such organisations are prompted by the need of safeguarding the trajectory of FDI by the World Bank and the MNCs. For the same reason, the latter are too choosy about the civil societies as their potential development collaborators in the developing countries. The New Economic Policy under the Structural Adjustment Programme as such believes in lowering down the density of interest group activities on the queer plea that, as Vieux and Petras pointed oujt, "economies with a lot of organisations have lower growth rates".[13] Mancor Olson, the political economist of structural adjustment, argues that these (growth of organisations) can be avoided chiefly, though not exclusively, by means of catastrophe, war and revolution. To him crisis and catastrophe are the key to breaking the inertia of civil society, as these disorient and weaken the interest groups.[14]

In one of their publications, Dreze and Sen boosted up the role of public action in economic development and in attaining social opportunities out of that. By public action they meant, local activism, social movement, pressure group activities, activism of the political organisations of the disadvantaged section and other forms of collective and community based actions by the local representative institutions such as village panchayats, women agencies and non-governmental public action.[15] But the contextual obsession let loose by globalisation in which public action would take place has remained conceptually unexplained and unattended by the authors. In fact public action has assumed a different connotation in the context of globalisation. In search of safe trajectory of FDI the World Bank has found the NGOs useful as they can be the link for reaching out to the people targeted for help.[16] The multinational organisations and the World Bank in the 1990s have opened up new avenues of collaboration with the civil society organisations, hitherto ignored, in the third world countries. The NGO Working Group of the World Bank (NGOWC) is an NGO forum for dialogue and advocacy among the NGOs and the World Bank. It was formed in 1984 with 23 member NGOs from every major region of the world in the Global Committee. NGOWC's central role is to act as a formal setting to address southern voices. In the Second Asia Pacific Regional Meeting of the NGOWC and the World Bank, the latter found collaboration with NGOs useful on the following considerations :

- Ensure long term sustainability of development projects through focusing on process approach.
- Input the NGO and civil society can provide with their knowledge and experience in development.
- NGOs and civil society can be the link for the multilateral institutions and World Bank to reach the people.
- NGOs and civil society can set critical issues in infrastructure development including environmental degradation, displacement and social cost in infrastructure development.
- Setting the normative issues in development initiative with civil society and NGOs to thrash out *'a common agenda of action'*.
- Efficient service delivery in reaching the poor effectively, in providing mechanisms for decentralisation, in evolving innovative approaches, in ensuring accountability and in strengthening democratic rights.[17]

On the other hand, the view of the NGOWC in collaborating with the World Bank was that they would be able to influence policy issues, instrumentalise their role in economic reform with a human face and be able to participate in policy and project works.[18]

The World Bank however did not provide a blanket patronage to the concept of collaboration with the civil society in the FDI programme. In a befitting manner the World Bank has imposed 'institutional conditionality' while providing aid, development grant and technical support. Institutions here mean not only the bureaucracy, but also the non-governmental organisations and the private sector. Considering that the local institutional capacity is often too weak to implement policy interventions,[19] the solution advocated by the World Bank is to help the governments by supporting initiatives from non-governmental organisations and local community and by involving the private sector.[20]

As such the World Bank has considered it unproductive to go in for foreign aid and loan below the market rate to the countries with weak institutions. The World Bank made it that it would provide assistance to those countries with stronger institutional performance and that the countries with sub-standard governance should not receive assistance from the international community.[21] Such institutional conditionality has become *sine qua non* to many foreign funding agencies which provide bilateral development grant to the NGOs in the developing countries.[22]

This is relevant in the context of key developments in India in the 1990s. A need has emerged at the grassroots NGOs level to restructure themselves in terms of Organisation Development, HRD, Inter-personal skill, Organisational Learning and Renewal, Institutional Restructuring and sectoral level clarity of NGOs.[23]

The World Bank stressed that NGOs will need to "reconcile their more traditional campaigning and advocacy role with their emerging role as partners with governments and industry in support of sustainable development."[24]

In the above background in the next part of the dissertation a case study of a World Bank aided "Assam Rural Infrastructure and Agriculture Services Project" is attempted.

III. A BRIEF APPRAISAL OF THE PROJECT

Assam Rural Infrastructure and Agricultural Services Project is a World Bank sponsored project. The major objectives of the project are :

(a) Improve equity and alleviation of poverty by offering better opportunities for farmers and women to contribute to agricultural growth and income generation.
(b) Improve nutrition of the poor.
(c) Accelerate agricultural growth through improved use of resources, relieving infrastructure, technical constraints and providing an enabling environment to facilitate the growth of private sector investment.
(d) Encourage sustainability of resources use and quality of environment.

(e) Improve Government of Assam's long term capacity for agricultural planning.

The project activities include fisheries, horticulture and livestock development. This project would benefit 3,00,000 poor rural people by increasing average annual net income from farming alone by 60 per cent and would create community asset and rural infrastructure, create 75 million man-days in infrastructure building and would increase nutritional status of the poor. The cost involvement of the project is US$ 126.0 million.[25]

The Globalisation Policy

The rationale for involvement of the World Bank in this project has been twofold.

(i) The project is consistent with Country Assistance Strategy (CAS) for India. CAS emphasises on direct support for specific reforms through policy-based investment operation at the sectoral, state and economy-wide levels.
(ii) CAS places increased importance on private sector initiatives and responsibility through encouraging private sector to supply goods and services, now provided exclusively by the public sector.[26]

Government of India's agricultural strategy has been tuned with the liberalization policy. While it includes development of area-specific assets and infrastructure required to support production and sustainable farming systems, plan and execute relevant research, extension and training programme for accelerating agricultural growth, the entire thrust has been to create a favourable policy and investment framework and an enabling environment for active private sector participation.

Government of Assam's agricultural development strategy has been formulated on these lines. This includes :

(i) Reduction of public sector delivery of production, inputs and services;
(ii) Introduction of cost recovery where possible and reduction of subsidies;
(iii) Diversification of farming towards products in which the state has comparative advantage;
(iv) Liberalization of the state trade policy;
(v) Preparation and implementation of demand-driven agricultural

research programme;

(vi) Introduction of policy incentives to promote private sector involvement in agriculture.[27]

In the area of globalization the positivistic role of the so-called welfare state as providers of goods and services is being rapidly replaced by indirect policy support in terms of creating an atmosphere conducive to FDI. The focus has shifted to creating a policy environment for that. The policy matrix of Government of Assam has been prepared accordingly. It has opened up a clean trajectory of FDI through this World Bank supported project.[28]

In the following part, the nature of involvement of local NGOs and people's organisations in the World Bank project in Assam is examined. As such, the project visualizes four major risks and intends to involve the former to reduce these risks :

1. *Funding* : To reduce the risk in funding, Government of Assam would submit an annual budget and commit to improve cost recovery by establishing adequate financial mechanisms. The pace of implementation, quality of construction and delivery of services would be monitored by local NGOs and be reported to concerned agencies every six months.
2. *Policy Reform and Commitment* : Adherence to policy reforms by Government of Assam has been assured in the policy matrix.
3. *Institutional Capacity* : The project document feels that success of the project depends upon active participation of local and national NGOs. It is an apprehension that government bureaucracy might delay the transfer of assets to the farming community. Such a participation would check bureaucratic delay.
4. *Security* : The security situation in Assam might delay field visits, timely supervision and monitoring. Project activities and investment programmes would be restricted to areas where security problems are minimal. Active involvement of the beneficiaries (FMC, WUA etc.) in the decision making process and their ownership to the project could reduce security risks.[29]

Involvement of NGOs and people's organisations in risk mitigation in four major areas as shown above, has got a few implications :

1. The World Bank intends to insulate itself from the society in which

its finance capital works. This may be called "secessionism of the rich" as Patnaik puts it.[30] The NGOs and the people's organisations, in such a context, have come to provide the insulation mechanism.

2. The term "security risk" has a greater implication. Beneficiary/people's organisation/NGO involvement in reducing security risk would further insulate the common mass, people's organisations and the NGO from the greater society as they would operate only and strictly within the security-trenched project area and the so-called target population.
3. The institutional questions implicating the NGOs are very subtle in the said project. While the credentials needed for the selection of NGOs are quite normal apparently, the hidden credential is that they must have institutional strength to reduce security risks. In another document of the World Bank, the hidden credential is exposed. "NGOs have a responsibility to be a part of the solution : the challenges of sustainable development in the sectors of interest".[31]
4. Participatory techniques for reducing security risks and conflict resolution brings us back to a very fundamental conceptual hiatus between behavioural (participatory) and structural approaches to conflict resolution. Given the fact that global capital rests on fundamental and irreconcilable inequality between the regions, nations and people, there is no reason to believe that conflicts and challenges created by it could be met by the behavioural method alone. On the other hand, given that the roots of conflict (security risk) is structural, the conflicts would invariably assume a strict political character which the NGOs or for that matter FMCs at large, cannot address from a social front alone and the behavioural approach to conflict resolution is invariably to give way. And still, if the NGOs and FMCs are to go for containment of potential conflicts and security risks, the former cannot but assume willy nilly a distinct political character. The FMCs have however been defined by the World Bank as *non-political village voluntary social groups* (italics mine) working for the welfare of economic growth of the village communities. The Department of Agriculture has actively promoted formation of FMCs to accelerate agricultural growth.[32] This would be contradiction of terms on the objective plane.
5. The role of FMCs and NGOs has been made instrumental in seeking a safe trajectory of world bank investment.

It can be mentioned that the *promotional character* of the NGOs and FMCs make them parasitic having no deep-rooted bases in the rural community in which they operate. Their role in conflict resolution is more a kind of policing role than anything else.

Project Implementation Plan

The attenuating need arising out of *'security risk'* calls for participation in selection, location, design and implementation of project activities. FMCs, WUAs and NGOs have been given responsibility for field level implementation of project activities including O & M of the common assets created thereby. The project management would however be guided by senior policy makers of the state who would be supported by NGO representatives. While the Line Department would implement project field activities, the Agricultural Production Commissioner would coordinate at state level. The possible areas where the NGO assistance would be required are :

Roads

Maintenance and afforestation/cultivation of roadside government land.

Irrigation

Assists in construction of STW through FMC, carry out rehabilitation of DTW surface irrigation scheme, repair and maintenance of pumps, assist farmers in selection and purchase of pumps and pipes and act as contractors for installation of STW on competitive basis.

The contractual role given by the World Bank project to the NGOs strips off the non-profit character of the latter.

Rice Based Farming Systems

Undertake farming on leased lands; practice participatory diagnostic research on farming systems and organise training for VLEW; provide short term orientation course for volunteer Extension Workers; assist in organising supply of seeds, fertilizers and pesticides; organise or assist in organising repair services for farm implements.

Horticulture

Raise nurseries on community or leased lands; develop horticulture on leased lands; provide training for food processing specially fruit processing; organise horticultural demonstrations; organise training and provide support to VLEWs; organise or assist in organising supply of planting materials and other inputs and assist in marketing of horticultural crops.

Fisheries

Develop fisheries in community tanks and bills; carry out demonstration of pond fisheries; provide extension service for starting pond fisheries; organise or assist in organising supply of fish seeds/fingerlings, nutrients and marketing.

Livestock and Fodder Development

Assist in fodder development on community lands; prepare demonstrations, specially for piggery; organise training and provide support to self-employed extension workers and fodder seed collection and marketing.

Other Innovative Activities

Practice organic farming and integrated pest management; carry out agricultural trials; prepare demonstration; pilot low cost irrigation such as the use of 'Zama' pumps, treadle pumps, ring wells etc.[33]

Besides, involvement of NGOs and FMCs has been sought in institutional development. The extension strategy of the project would be to strengthening the role of contact farmers and group approaches through stronger link with FMCs and NGOs, to develop extension materials for women farmers, to use local mass media and to expand participation of field staff and NGOs.[34]

Project Organisation and Management

The Agricultural Production Commissioner (APC) would coordinate and guide all the departments and agencies in implementing the project activities. Each implementing department or agency would identify one officer responsible for coordinating all its activities under the project. To assist the APC, a Project Implementation Unit (PIU) headed by a Director and supported by two Economists, one Environmentalist, one Anthropologist and an Accounts Officer, would be established.

The PIU would include an NGO and environmental cell to coordinate beneficiary participation. To assist the implementation, two committees would be set up as below :

I. Project Guidance Committee (PGC), headed by the Chief Secretary of the state. The APC would serve as secretary to PGC. Other senior secretaries and four NGO representatives would serve as members. This committee would approve the project annual plan.

II. Project Coordination Committee (PCC) would include APC as committee chairperson, the Project Director as its secretary, heads of implementing departments and agencies, Additional Secretary (Finance) of the mini secretariat and representative of NGOs and User Groups as members. The PCC would review annual work plan and associated expenditures in the budget prepared by PIU prior to submission to the PGC for approval. It would periodically assess project performance and offer suggestions for implementation.

The respective Line departments, the district and block development administration and the state agricultural university would undertake the implementation of project activities. Participation of the NGO and beneficiaries would be ensured through their representation in the separate terms created in each Line department.

The DCs would coordinate and integrate all project activities in the district and assist the APC and Project Director in planning and overseeing implementation. The BDO would perform similar role at the block level. At the district, block and village levels, the District Planning and Development Council, the Panchayat Samiti and the Village Panchayats would help the rural development administration in planning and implementing project activities. These local institutions would be important contact points for communicating with people and sensitising them to project activities.

The environmentalist in the PIU would carry out environmental assessment and ameliorating activities. The expert would organise workshops as forum for NGOs and others to deliberate on all aspects of the project. At these workshops, the NGO representatives would be elected to various committees.

The Anthropologist in the PIU would coordinate with NGO activities, specifically reviewing investment proposals with respect to the participatory process and social concerns; developing innovative proposals for possible implementation under the project; standardising methodology, procedure and norms for major field activities and monitoring and evaluating NGO activities implemented with financial assistance from the project.

The NGO and Environment Cell would also develop and implement guidelines for monitoring activities throughout the project.[35]

Planning Procedure

The economist of the PIU would formulate the annual programme in consultation with the heads of the departments/agencies, DCs and NGOs. It would also review implementation programme during the year, review the M & E reports, other specific studies and NGO/beneficiary suggestions as the basis of project planning.[36]

Conclusion

The dominance of finance capital has set in a process of World Bank-Civil Society alliance whereby the latter is thoroughly oriented by the ideology of finance capital. The project management plan has gone one step further by implicating the Panchayat bodies. It is worthwhile to mention in this connection that the Government of India in the 1990s has taken two ventures. One, liberalising the country's economy and two, empowering the Panchayat Raj institutions through the 73rd Amendment of the Constitution of India. The contextual obsession in which the Act was passed is significant. Apparently though the two ventures stand at polar opposite philosophical premises — one at capital and the other at people — the subtle link between the two ventures cannot be simply wished away. Empowering the Panchayati Raj institutions is a part of the liberalisation programme. It is to provide institutional conditionality as required by the policy of liberalisation. Both the civil society and the local governance institutions would, in this situation, provide indigenous mechanisms for risk management and the Panchayati bodies would become comprador to the World Bank rather than authentic grassroots institutions. In the bandwagon of globalisation the tall claim of poverty alleviation as stated in the project document, is a seer violence to the objective reality of finance capital. The entire proposition is based on fundamental contradiction of capital and labour. The intellectual commitment sought from the anthropologists would also snatch the independence with which the astute anthropologists of this region have served the people after the Independence of the country. The role of NGOs in ensuring beneficiary participation in a situation of seclusion from the mass would be a major hoax.

The current intellectual discourses on civil society in India have been initiated in the context of globalisation. The discourse evolves round two major themes — strengthening autonomy of intermediary institutions (Beteille) on the one hand and revivalism of traditional civil society (Kothari, Nandy) on the other. Beteille stressed upon institutional efficiency of the intermediary institutions wherein drive of experts, not aspirations of individuals would find place. Kothari while acknowledging the fact of deinstitutionalisation (which is the result of growing lack of fit between government institutions and social demand),[37] advocated invigoration of civil society with the tradition which need to be built in the changed historical context.[38] According to Kothari, "liberalisation is not to be a goal to be achieved but a game to be played out to permanently subjugate both the autonomy of the state and the autonomy of the civil society.[39] He stressed upon the "need to pick up the threads once again to join them to the new resurgence at the grassroots and the multiple stirrings of the human conscience that are already under way, and produce a new agenda of human conscience.[40] While Beteille tended to build up civil society on current globalisation context, Kothari tended towards an introspection into the past. It may be mentioned here that while in the West civil society was a brake from the past, Kothari believes in going back to the past.[41] To both Beteille and Kothari the question is: does civil society exist in its own rights (given either 'institutional efficiency' or 'invigoration') in the globalisation context in which the debate over the civil society is taking place? The content of this dissertation is that civil society is thoroughly a domain of the bourgeois and even if the former has come to exist with apparent autonomy, it has never been free from the context in which it emerged. Hence it is as unfree as ever. Yet if the so-called civil societies through efficiency animation or through invigoration come forward to play a protective force against exploitation, as many people still think, they can do so *only after* shedding their so-called civil character and simultaneous assumption of a clean political character. The current liberal country discourse on civil society seems to avoid this fact.

NOTES

1. John Keane (ed.), *Civil Society and the State.* Verso. London 1988.
2. *Ibid.*

In the 18th century Adam Smith was the greatest champion of market economy whereby reasonable men pursued wealth through individual self-interest. Smith intended to liberate trade and exchange from the dictates of mercantilist state and the trappings of feudalism and to lay those on the principle of *laissez faire*. Thus to Smith, civil society stood in opposition to the state. Scot Adam Ferguison, Smith's follower, in his 'Essays on the History of Civil Society' noted, 'civilizing trends' in modern societies. To him, under this system of economy there was expansion of manufacturing, improvement of technology, cost reduction and profit rise, moderated conflicts commercial growth. Ferguison's view was shaped by the changes in the 18th century Scotland in his day whereby the two civilizations divided the 18th century Scotland — Gemeinscaft of the clan and Gesselscaft of the progressive commercial low lands." (Jamie Swift, Civil Society in Question. Between the Lines, Canada, 1999).

3. C.A. Vaughan, *History of Political Philosophy.*
4. Bertrand Russel, *History of Western Philosophy.*
5. Gurpreet Mahajan, Civil Society and its Avtars, *EPW,* May 15, 1999.
6. *Ibid.*
7. Joseph O Malley (ed.), Critique of Hegel's Philosophy of Rights. *CUP,* 1979.
8. Marx and Engels, *German Ideology.* Progress Publishers, Moscow, 1964.
9. Jamie Swift, *Civil Society in Question, Between the Lines.* Canada. 1999. Also see Neera Chandhok, *"State and Civil Society - Explorations in Political Theory".* Sage, 1995.
10. Ajit Roy, Civil Society and Nation State in the Context of Globalisation. *EPW,* August 5-12, 1995.
11. Mahajan, *op. cit.*
12. Sharon M. Oster, Strategic Management of Non Profit Organizations — Theory and Cases. *OUP,* 1995.
13. Steve Vieux and James Petras, Selling Structural Adjustment — Intellectuals in Uniform, *EPW,* January 1996.
14. *Ibid.*
15. Jean Dreze and Amartya Sen, India — Economic Development and Social Opportunities, *OUP,* 1996.
16. S. Swaminathan, World Bank and NGOs. *Hindu,* November 1, 1996. "The World Bank acknowledges that the NGOs have played a crucial role in developing the concept of, and fostering support for, sustainable development. Their advocacy for environmental social issues serves to balance the proponents of development, regardless of consequences. However, international and local NGOs that subscribe to social objectives, also have a responsibility to accurately reflect the desire of the communities they represent...." (Kathryn McPhail and Aiden Davy, Integrating Social Concerns into Private Sector Decision Making. *World Bank Discussion Paper 384* Washington DC.)
17. Second Asia Pacific Regional Meeting of NGOWC — A Summary Report *Global Alliance News.* Society for Participatory Research in Asia, New Delhi, June 1996.
18. *Ibid.*
19. Commenting on community dynamics of institutional reforms R.E. Lope stated, "although economics has lot to say about the motivation for discard

ing the old institutions and replacing them by new, usually more efficient ones, there are a number of factors delaying and even postponing the adoption of socially desirable institutions :

Failure to perceive the relationship between the stock of natural resources and the flows of extracted resources; old institutions have become part of group's cultural heritage whereby deviation is associated with social reprisal, even if they are no longer efficient as population increases; high value placed on equity in spite of social disparities in poor agrarian societies; homogeneity among rural poor; communal ownership of land and land abundance.

Lopez was of the opinion that collective action for management of common property is likely to fail as the conditions on which such collective action depends are not always present in poor rural communities. (R.E. Lopez, Where Development can or cannot go — The Role of Poverty Environment Linkages. *Annual World Bank Conference on Development Economics,* (eds) Borris Plescovic & J.E. Stiglitz. The World Bank. Washington D.C. 1977.)

Lopez in his craze for legitimising privatisation, failed to grasp the dynamics of old institutions. He failed to look into the high degree of efficiency of the old institutions in facing the challenges posed by the decline of CPR and also in facing those external agencies to destroy the same. Lopez put forward only one factor — i.e. population increase responsible for reduced stock of natural resources overlooking the long hands of eco-colonialism — the role of timber forest merchandise in steady natural resource depletion particularly in the South Asian, African and Latin American countries. The instances of efficient local institutions in preserving CPR are many. In the North-East India, the confederacy of Mao clan is still the chief owner of land. The Khasi matrimony is still the repository of CPR. It is a note to Lopez that in the north-eastern region, it is not the demographic pressure *per se,* but increasing commercialisation, of CPR that is responsible for resource depletion.

20. Alberto Alesina, The Political Economy of High and Low Growth. *Annual World Bank Conference on Development Economics. Ibid.*
21. *Ibid.*
22. New Zealand Overseas Development Agency's "Good Governance Programme" floated through the Ministry of External Affairs in 1998, New Zealand.
23. Ranjani K. Murthy and Mallika Singh, Training, Organisational Development and Sectoral Strengthening Need of NGOs in India. *Search Bulletin XII(I).* Bangalore. 1997.
24. Kathryn McPhail and Aiden Davy, Integrating Social Concerns into Private Sectors Decision Making. *World Bank Discussion Paper 384.* Washington DC.
25. Document of the World Bank Report No. 13888 - IN. *Staff Appraisal Report* — India — Assam Rural Infrastructure and Agricultural Project, April 26, 1995. World Bank.
26. *Ibid.*

27. *Ibid.*
28. Policy Matrix of Government of Assam. Document of the World Bank. *Ibid.*
29. Document of the World Bank. *Ibid.*
30. Prabhat Patnaik, Nation State in the Era of Globalisation, *EPW,* August 19, 1995.
    In the World Conference on Injury Prevention and Control by WHO, Dr. Emannuel Rozental Klinger held in March 2000, stated that "the ethics of interpersonal relationship are altered under the circumstances of poverty. Social exclusion within contexts characterised by inequality and poverty is fertile ground for all kinds of violence." *The Hindustan Times,* March, 8. 2000.
31. Kathryn McPhail and Aiden Davy, *op. cit.*
32. Document of the World Bank. *op. cit.*
33. *Ibid.*
34. *Ibid.*
35. *Ibid.*
36. *Ibid.*
37. Rajni Kothari, Globalisation and Revival of Tradition - Dual Attack on Model of Democratic Nation Building. *EPW,* March 25, 1995.
38. Dipankar Gupta, Civil Society or the State: What Happened to Citizenship", In Ramchandra Guha and Jonathan Parry (eds.) Institutions and Inequality: Essays in Honour of Andre Beteille. *OUP,* 1999.
39. Rajni Kothari, *op. cit.*
40. *Ibid.*
41. Dipankar Gupta, *op. cit.*

8

INTEGRATED MANAGEMENT OF NATURAL RESOURCES OF NORTH-EAST INDIA FOR SUSTAINABLE DEVELOPMENT IN 21ST CENTURY

A. K. Mishra

Human beings are heavily dependant on natural resources for their very survival. Natural resources of all kinds, particularly water, soil, forest, vegetation (flora) and animals (fauna) are the major resource base supporting and sustaining the human and cattle population. As a result of exploding population, the pressure on limited natural resources has increased immensely. With an additional burden of population, the requirement of water, food, fibre, shelter and other essential commodities are expected to grow almost double or triple in next century. Already, the resources are facing serious threat due to overexploitation, unplanned, unscientific and haphazard developmental activities associated with mismanagement in North-East India. The situation is expected to only become worse which will jeopardise the resource sustainability.

Careful utilization avoiding the overuse/misuse or wastage and integrated management of natural resources on watershed basis assuring the people's participation will form the basis for success in the endeavours of resources conservation and sustainability with developmental objectives of North-East India in next millennium. The present write up attempts to critically evaluate the status of resources availability, future demand, potentials for development and harnessing, and also tries to suggest ways and means of exploiting the natural resources for sustainability towards the development of North-East India in 21st century.

Introduction

"Centuries ago, an ancient civilization defined the earth creating gods for the air, the sea, the wind, for fire and water and for the earth itself. For hundreds of thousands of years humanity lived in harmony with the planet. In the milliseconds that represents the last two hundred years in the life of the earth, we stand poised to distort it."

— Goldsmith, *et al.*, (1990)

The above statement of a great thinker of modern times in a famous book on environmental conservation and management by the author, *"5000 Days to Save the Planet"*, poses a very serious and a very simple question to its readers, as to whether we want to live in harmony with the nature, as we the mankind, have been doing it from centuries and transfer this great heritage to our next generations or to irrecoverably damage and distort the same so that it should become a great curse on them? Already much damage has been done to the *Only One Earth* that we have to live upon. There is very limited period left before us to decide and act. It is not that any body has showed this type of concern only recently but there were people who have expressed similar thoughts in past too, e.g.

> "We are living today in a society frightened by what is happening to its environment.. Progress..., appears to many people to have resulted either to a situation in which far reaching technical developments are initiated without adequate understanding of their ramifications, or worse, to the deliberate acceptance of procedures known to be unsatisfactory simply because they are cheap and easy to implement. The result is a rapid deterioration in the quality of the human environment."
>
> — Black (1969)

These words were written over 20 years ago when the word *"Sustainability"* itself was non-existent. Either, they did not belong to Brundtland Commission report or are from one of the many reviews of the sustainability. However, these lines are a reminder to us the anxiety about sustaining the environment from many human activities and had been expressed long before the word *Sustainability* was coined which subsequently became the common currency of the world.

The Concept of Sustainable Development

A definition of sustainable developments that of Bruntland Commission,

F.A.O., says that —

> *"...Development which meets the need of the current generation without jeopardizing the needs of future generations."*

> According to another definition of sustainable development :

> "Sustainable development is the management and conservation of the natural resource base and the orientation of technological and institutional changes in such a manner as to ensure the attainment and continued satisfaction of human needs for present and future generation. Such sustainable development in the agriculture, forestry and fishery sector, conserves land, water and animal genetic resources is environmentally degradable, technologically appropriate, economically viable and socially acceptable."
>
> — Bruntland Commission, F.A.O., U.N., Rome

Amidst the global concern to save the earth and its resources the mountain and hill natural resources which form a sizeable portion of the whole, stand as a big question mark as far as the conservation, development and management of these resources are concerned. For sustainable development of mountainous region, integrated and environmentally sustainable development strategies have become inevitable for planning these days. Natural resources management in the context of mountain environment necessitate proper planning strategies. Such resources primarily include soil, water and vegetation. The other parameters that have bearing on the genesis and pattern of the resources are geology, climate, topography, relief, aspect of slope of a region etc.

Eastern Himalayan region is one of the most geo-dynamically unstable, ecologically sensitive and economically underdeveloped mountain range of the world. The unpredictable land transformation processes operating in these tectonically active and geographically critical fold mountain tracts has led the region to a highly vulnerable state. Also, the uncontrolled and unabated exploitation of natural resources could lead the region to a most disastrous future that would have major adverse effect on the ecological balance and the socio-economic welfare of large communities inhabiting in the region and its surroundings.

North-Eastern India

The North-East India or the North-Eastern Himalayan Region, a part of the Lesser Himalayas, are the most densely populated part of the entire Himalayan mountain range deserving adequate and specific attention for conservation, development and management of its precious natural resources sustaining all forms of animal and vegetative life. Because the land is a complex of soil, water and vegetation and other productive resources upon which all terrestrial bio-systems are dependant, the need to conserve and manage the valuable natural resources of the region is now increasingly realized (Bisht and Tiwari, 1996). The need for sustainable development of mountainous region, therefore, makes it imperative to adopt a comprehensive land and water use policy, exploitation of mountain flora and forest, underground mineral resources etc. based on scientific principles and planned management and frequent monitoring of the whole range of the mountain natural resources.

Location, Physiography and Climatology

The North-Eastern region of India, situated between 21° 51' and 29°39' N latitudes land 88° 40' to 97° 31' E longitudes, comprises of eight states, i.e. Arunachal Pradesh, Assam, Manipur, Meghalaya, Mizoram, Nagaland, Sikkim, Tripura and three districts of West Bengal, viz. Darjeeling, Jalpaiguri and Cooch-Behar. The region has the total geographical area of 275 thousand km^2 of which 212 thousand km^2 is in hills having an altitude range of 60-3000 feet above mean sea level (m.s.l.). The topography of the region is a mixture of moderately high to high hills and deep gullies in hilly states and two hill districts of Assam and valleys of Brahmaputra and Barak rivers. The region has mainly been divided into three major physiographic zones viz. (a) Hills and mountains, (b) peninsular plateau and (c) the plains (Sharma and Sarma, 1991). Accordingly, the climate varies from near tropical in the plains to alpine in the hills. However, for more efficient management the Eastern Himalayan region has been subdivided into 5 sub-regions, viz., (i) Sikkim and Darjeeling, (ii) A.P., Meghalaya, Nagaland and North Cachar of Assam, (iii) Manipur, Nagaland and Mizoram, (iv) Assam South and (v) Most of Assam, Jalpaiguri and Cooch-Behar districts of W.B. Hills and mountains of folded topography characterize the region (Basu and Guha, 1996). The soils of the region are usually rich in organic matter (over one per cent) and acidic in reaction. The soil pH ranges from 4.0 to 5.5 (Prasad *et al.,* 1981). The low soil pH is attributed to leaching of salts under the influence of heavy rainfall. On an average about 63 per cent of the area is under forest of various types. The region is ecologically suitable for forestry, livestock production, and horticulture and to the limited extent for many developmental effort with proper natural resources management. This is vital for economic upliftment of Himalayan people and to achieve environmental protection of the typically fragile ecosystem in Eastern Himalayan region.

Natural Resource of the North-East India : An Inventory

The region has been endowed with abundant natural resources of all kinds. Therefore, it has been rightly characterized as one of the "Megadiversity Zones" owing to its rich and diverse potential of soil, water, vegetation and bio-diversity. Indiscriminate and reckless exploitation of the natural resources combined with mismanagement due to the process of development, urban settlement, *Jhuming* and other economic activities of rapidly rising population has brought the region to acute resources crunch. The region has become highly vulnerable and disbalanced in its natural wealth. Land and water, two basic and most vital natural resources, sustaining all forms of life are facing serious problems of degradation and depletion due to mismanagement in the North Eastern Hill region (Mishra and Gupta, 1998). The exploitation of these resources in highly unplanned and unscientific manner has resulted into serious problems of soil erosion, loss of soil fertility by washing off and leaching of essential nutrients, degradation of steep hill slopes, siltation of river beds and reservoirs, thus, loss of reservoir storage capacity, recurrence of menacing floods in valley regions resulting into heavy loss of lives and property every year, extinction of rarest species of flora and fauna, wastage of enormous amount of safe and good quality water, decreasing average annual rainfall and shifting of monsoon patterns, practice of mono-cropping due to unavailability of water in the post-monsoon season consequently, low productivity of crops, and a variety of other associated problems related to environment and ecology. The dimension of the above problems is much higher in this region mainly due to the high average annual rainfall and rugged topography of the region because steep slopes are more prone to erosion (Sharma and Mishra, 1998).

Human Resource

The North-Eastern Himalayan region of India is inhabited by a large number of tribes who have got diverse traditions and separate ethnic culture. The population of the region as per 1991 census was 31,547,314 (Anonymous,1992). The change in growth rate of the population during the period 1971-81 to 1981-91 is +1.68, -11.81, -3.17, +0.82, -8.85, +6.03 and +2.38

per cent for Arunachal Pradesh, Assam, Manipur, Meghalaya, Mizoram, Nagaland and Tripura, respectively. Average annual expected growth rate for the decade 1981-91 was +2.71% (Anonymous, 1995). However, it is interesting to find out that while population in this region could hardly double over a period of 50 years from 1901 to 1951, it doubled during the next 20 years (between 1951-1971). Between 1971 and 1981 we find that the rate of growth of population in the NE region has been almost double that of the all-India population growth rate (Mahajan, 1987). With the mounting population pressure of such high rate and the changed scenario of growth and development the processes causing the extensive damage to the natural resources have hastened manifold in the North- Eastern Himalayan region of India.

Natural Resources

All types of natural resources can broadly be characterized into two major groups; renewable and non-renewable. A potentially renewable resource is one that can be depleted in the short run if used or polluted too rapidly but ultimately it is replaced through natural processes, e.g. trees in forest, grasses, wild animals, fresh surface water, fresh air and fertile soil. The highest rate at which a resource can be used without decreasing its full potential for renewal throughout the world or in a particular area is called its *natural replacement rate or sustainable yield.* If these yields exceeded the base supply, a renewable resource begins to shrink — a process known as environmental degradation. Although, the region is highly rich in all types of natural resources, viz. flora, fauna, minerals, different types of micro climates, different topographical settings, various ethnic groups, cultures, land and water resources etc.; yet our present discussion will be centered around the conservation and efficient management of two most vital and important natural resources, i.e. soil and water.

Soil and Water Resources of the North-Eastern Himalayan Region

The North-Eastern Region (including Sikkim, Darjeeling and New Jalpaiguri Districts of W.B.) states have total geographical area 262 thousand km^2 of which 212 thousand km^2 is in hills. Arunachal Pradesh is the largest state, having 83,740 km^2 area while Sikkim is the smallest, state of the region with the geographical area of 7096 km^2. Assam has the maximum net sown area whereas, Mizoram has the minimum (27,060 km^2 and 650 km^2, respectively) (Anonymous, 1995). Rice is the major crop of the region. It accounts for approximately 90 per cent of the area and 92 per cent of production under total foodgrains. The other major crops are maize, wheat, millets, oilseeds and pulses. Different cropping systems for different agro-climatic zones have been designed by experts along with input management for higher yields and ensuring food security but the tribal farmer's response has been lukewarm in this regard. So much so the experts now think that the shifting cultivation cannot be replaced but it can only be suitably modified as per the need of farmers and as per the agroclimatologic settings of a zone (Ramakrishna, 1990; Borthakur, 1998; Lal, 1998; Singh, 1998; Mishra and Gupta, 1998).

The Forest Resources

The region has 167.4 thousand km^2 area under forests which constitutes approximately 63.9 per cent of the total geographical area is under cover of various types (Table 8.1). The dense forest cover (crown density 40 per cent or more) is only about 91.2 thousand km^2 (34.8 %) and 76.2 thousand km^2 (29.09 %) is open forest area (crown density 10-40%). Nagaland and Arunachal Pradesh have 88.12 and 82.0 per cent of its total geographical area under forest of one type or other respectively, whereas Assam has only 30.6 per cent of its geographical area under forests (Anonymous, 1997). There are broadly four categories of forests in the region based on the ownership patterns, viz. government, civil, corporate bodies and private. Arunachal Pradesh and Assam have maximum forest area under government control, while Meghalaya has maximum forest area under private ownership. Several species of grasses and shrubs are found in the region. Important forest species found in the region are *Dendrocalamus humiltoni, Gmelina arborea, Shorea robusta, Vitex penduncularis, Terminalia belerica, Emblica officnalis, Schima wallichii, Bauhinia pupurea* etc. Because of this the region is considered as mega-biodiversity area. However, due to indiscriminate deforestation the forests of the region have started dwindling at an annual rate of 0.7 per cent in the region. The deforestation, which includes the cutting of agricultural terraces on steeper and more marginal slopes, has led to a catastrophic increase in soil erosion and loss of productive land through accelerated landslide incidences, and to disruption of normal hydrologic cycle. The situation in turn has led to increased runoff during summer monsoon and increase in disastrous flooding and massive siltation in the plains, and lower water levels and drying up of springs and wells during the dry season. Related ills are rapid siltation of reservoirs, abrupt changes in the course of rivers, spread of barren sand and gravel across rich agricultural areas in the course of the rivers on the plains, and increased incidences of diseases in the downstream areas. The continuous loss of agricultural lands in the mountains leads to another round of deforestation to enable the construction of more terraces on which to grow subsistence crops. Yet, as the labour of walking greater distances from the village to the fuel wood supplies increases with the receding forest perimeter, a critical threshold is reached whereby the available human energy (principally females) becomes professionally over taxed and an increasing quantity of another vicious circle is linked to the first one. Terrace soils are deprived of natural fertilizer as the animal dung now is increasingly used for fuel, thus depriving the agricultural tracts their due share of organic manure. In many instances the dung is the only source of fertilizer. The lower crop yields weakens soil structure that further augments the incidences of landslides. The diminishing forest cover has resulted in the changed rainfall pattern and other climatic variables.

Table 8.1 : Geographical area and forest cover in North-Eastern India (in km²)

States	Geogra. Area (km²)	Recorded Forest Cover	%of Geogra. Area	Actual Forest Cover	%of Geogra. Area
Arunachal Pradesh	83621	51540	61.63	68621	82.06
Assam	78438	30708	39.15	24061	30.68
Manipur	22327	15154	67.87	17558	78.64
Meghalaya	22429	8514	42.34	15714	70.06
Mizoram	21081	15935	75.59	18576	88.12
Nagaland	165769	8625	52.005	14291	85.59
Tripura	10486	6309	60.00	5538	52.81
Sikkim	7096	2650	37.35	3127	44.07
Total	262057	140104	53.46	167486	63.91

Source : Anonymous, 1997.

Notes : 1. Recorded forest area is land classified as forest irrespective of the actual status.
2. Percentage deviation of actual from the recorded is negative.

The effect of large-scale deforestation is found in checking the impact of the falling raindrops. The erosive kinetic energy of the falling raindrops which used to be checked from the extensive vegetal cover is no more intercepted and desiccated now as a result the large volume of water is crossing the boundary of the region as surface runoff. The monthly erosion index of some places in the region has been presented in Table 8.2.

The sheet erosion is no more being checked from the sparse vegetation on the hill slopes giving rise to rill and gully erosion streams. The rainwater that used to be retained as surface retention and detention and infiltration in deep layers of soil that used to appear as base flow in the minor springs and streams is no more available round the year affecting the people of this region. Consequently almost all the hill states of the region are suffering badly for the want of drinking water in the post-monsoon season keeping aside the other requirements and the crisis of potable water is worsening day by day. As all the problems in the nature are intrrelated and hence, are governed by the factors causing the problems there is an immediate need to immediately check and control the factors responsible for the damage to the natural systems.

Table 8.2 : Average monthly Erosion Index (EI) values (Metric Units)

Months	North Lakhimpur	Guwahati	Shillong	Imphal	Agartala
Jan.	0.5	—	—	—	2.8
Feb.	1.8	—	—	1.0	18.7
Mar.	6.2	5.6	4.8	1.3	39.8
Apr.	18.9	40.6	17.8	1.9	104.8
May.	102.5	74.2	55.4	42.7	282.1
Jun.	242.9	146.9	122.4	51.1	283.0
Jul.	288.6	149.5	56.7	38.2	203.2
Aug.	268.6	139.3	50.0	53.2	141.8
Sep.	200.5	65.7	84.7	20.2	122.9
Oct.	43.9	9.6	15.7	12.1	79.5
Nov.	5.1	3.7	—	1.2	2.0
Dec.	1.8	—	—	—	—
Annual	1181.0	635.4	407.5	228.2	1280.6

Source : Rambabu *et al.*, 1978.

Water Resources

Rainfall is the major source of all the water in this region. The North-Eastern region has been bestowed immensely by the nature as far as the rainfall is concerned. Some other forms of precipitation such as snowfall, hail, dew, fog etc. do occur at some places but the contribution from these forms of precipitation is negligibly small as compared to the rainfall. Normally this region is rated as the highest water availability region mainly due to excessive rainfall. Cherrapunjee and Mawsynram are the world famous places receiving the highest amounts of average annual rainfall of the order of approximately 11000 mm. The major portion of the annual rainfall in the region (about two-third) is received during the monsoon months of April-September. The seven North-Eastern states of the region, (excluding Sikkim) though have 7.75 per cent of the geographical area of the country receives about 11 per cent of the total precipitation of the country. Naturally, this high amount of rainfall will generate a sizeable amount of runoff owing to its topographical setting. The physiography of the region is such that it is crossed by innumerable number of rivulets, streams, and rivers and has two major drainage channels, viz. Brahmaputra and Barak. The catchment area of two major drainage lines, viz. Brahamaputra and Barak river systems around 194.4 and 78.1 thousand km^2, respectively. The total area covered by lakes, reservoirs and tanks are 91,256, 51,609 and 40,706 has, respectively.

River Basins

The rainfall of north-eastern region corresponds to about 510 km^3 water. The total water potential (ground water plus surface water) of the region has been estimated to be around 16.6 km^3 and 1064.7 km^3, respectively. The total length of major rivers in the region is 19,468 km. Brahmaputra and Barak rivers are two major natural drainage channels in the region which together drain an area of approximately 194,413 sq. km and 78,150 sq. km respectively in the states of Arunachal Pradesh, Assam, Meghalaya, Nagaland, Manipur, and southern Assam. Both river basins cover aproximately 86 per cent of the geographical area of the North Eastern region (Sharma, 1996). The Brahmaputra carries an annual flow of 61.65 million ha m and silt load of 3700 hectare metre (Anonymous, 1985). The river basin is geologically unstable, hydrologically dynamic, meteorologically extreme and seismologically dynamic and only about 10 per cent of the annual flow is economically harnessable (Hazarika, 1988). As the region is very prone to earthquakes of high intensities there is a scarcity of storage structures or sites in hills. The same region makes the region unfavourable for construction of large dams which in turn restricts harnessing of large volumes of good quality of water of Brahmaputra river. The high silt load carried by the river is one more factor for non-construction of large dams on the rivers — Brahmapautra and Barak. Per capita and per ha annual run-off from Brahmaputra and Barak basin has been presented in Table 8.3.

Table 8.3 : Water Availability from Major Rivers of North-Eastern Himalayan Region

River basins	Drainage Area (km^2)	Annual Runoff (M m^3)
Brahmaputra	194413	537240
Barak and Others	78150	59800
Total	272563	597040

Source : Anonymous (1995).

Total Water Potential

The water potential of various states of the region has been presented in Table 8.4. Assam has the highest surface water potential of 558,776 Mm^3 while Tripura has the lowest (7,616 Mm^3). The total groundwater and surface water potential of the region is 16.6 Mm^3 and 1064.7 Mm^3, respectively (Sharma, 1996). The approximate present annual demand for water is around 7.8 Mm^3 for domestic, agriculture, industrial, energy and other uses. The demand for water is expected to be 13.0 Mm^3 in 2010 AD and 19.2 Mm^3 in 2025 AD. About 64.1 per cent of the demand of water are for irrigation (Sharma and Mishra, 1998). The total water potential of North-East has been shown in Table-8.4.

Table 8.4 : Total Water Potential of North-Eastern States (Surface plus Ground Water)

State	Surface Water Potential (Mm^3)	Ground water Potential (Mm^3)	Irrigation Potential ('000 ha)	
			Major	Minor
Arunachal Pradesh	366000	787	NE	266
Assam	558776	14820	970	1700
Manipur	19794	44	135	105
Meghalaya	67216	357	20	100
Mizoram	31291	—	NE	80
Nagaland	14090	Neg.	10	80
Tripura	7616	588	100	115

Source : Anonymous (1995). NE = Not estimated

Irrigation Potential and Development

The ultimate irrigation potential of the region is 1235 thousand ha from major and medium project and 2446 thousand ha from minor projects. Assam has the highest ultimate irrigation potential of 2670 thousand ha from major and minor projects. Total irrigated area in the region is around 560,000 ha of which 69.8 per cent area is in Assam (Table 8.5). Manipur has 25.5 per cent of the net sown area under irrigation compared to 13.8 per cent in Meghalaya. Manipur has also the highest ultimate irrigation potential of 171.4 per cent of the net sown area. Due to hilly terrain, the development of major and medium irrigation projects is not economical, as the cost-benefit ratio of irrigation projects is unfavourable in this region. In such circumstances it is not very wise to let the rainwater escape from the place it falls. Rather various strategies should be followed for conservation, storage, *in situ* water harvesting etc. And efficient utilization and management of resources of the region need to be undertaken. The ground water extraction, creation of surface storage, water conservation tanks and *in situ*, improving irrigation efficiency and reduction in evaporation loss by judicious application of water is the need of hour. Since most of the area is hilly, development of agriculture based on micro-watershed approach will be more useful.

Table 8.5 : Irrigation Potential and Extent of Irrigation in North-Eastern States ('000 ha)

State	Irrigated Area	Ultimate Potential % as of NSA	Per cent of NSA Irrigated
Arunachal Pradesh	23	—	17.7
Assam	391	99.7	14.6
Manipur	34	171.4	25.5
Meghalaya	24	47.4	13.8
Mizoram	8	123.0	12.3
Nagaland	42	49.4	23.1
Tripura	38	87.4	15.6

Source : Anonymous (1995). NSA= Net Area Sown

Major Soil and Water Concerns

Soil erosion is very serious problem in the hilly region. Human activities related to the use and exploitation of natural resources for food production and other economic benefits have adverse effects in terms of land degradation. Land degradation is quite a crisis that is unfolding gradually in the hilly and mountainous regions. Within the Himalayan region, soil erosion from agricultural activities on slope lands has been, by and large, the major contributor to the land degradation. The loss of top soil has affected the ability to grow foods in two ways. First, it has reduced the inherent productivity of the land through both loss of nutrients and the degradation of other elements in the physical structure of the soil and second, it has also increased the cost of food production. There are many visible signs of the process of degradation and over-exploitation such as denuded and degraded hills, diminishing forest cover, the rocky and rugged barren terrain full of boulders and high sediment transport in the rainy season due to which the colour of water often becomes reddish. The other ill effects, invisible to naked eyes are apparent in the form of nutrient leaching and fertility erosion, loss of ecological diversity, shrinking lakes, and siltation of river beds and reservoirs etc. The other related ill effects which take long time to result in are shifting of the monsoon pattern, reduction in average annual rainfalls and climatic changes in the form of rise in the temperature etc. have also started showing slowly but steadily. The hydrological behaviour as affected by the human interference in the natural systems and the mismanagement of the natural resources is also changing rapidly. The total annual rainfall has started showing a declining trend and average number of dry spells in the region is on the increase (Mishra, 1998).

Land Use Pattern

The topography of North-Eastern Himalayan region is characterized by undulating hilly terrain. This limits the scope for utilization of water resources for irrigation. Rainfed agriculture is mostly practiced in the region following old traditional cultivation practices. Shifting Cultivation or *jhuming,* is the predominant form of agriculture widely prevalent in the North-Eastern Himalayan Region of India. Approximately an area of about 31.1 per cent of the total geographical area has been classified as wasteland in Assam followed by Manipur (25.3%). Only about 37,220 km^2 or 14.5 per cent of the total area is under cultivation in the region (including Sikkim) (Anonymous, 1985).

The annual area affected from shifting cultivation in different states varies from 19.0, 22.3, 53.0, 63.0, 69.6, 70.0, 90.0 thousand hectares in the states of Nagaland, Tripura, Meghalaya, Mizoram, Assam, Arunachal Pradesh and Manipur respectively (Prasad and Sharma, 1990). A sizeable amount of biomass including wet/dry leaves, forest litter and wooden material is burnt in uncontrolled conditions in this method (slash and burn) of agriculture (Mishra *et al.,* 1998). The system is highly uneconomical and has caused extensive resource depletion and widespread land and environmental degradation in the region (Ramkrishna, 1990).

The region is under severe threat of soil erosion mainly due to the shifting cultivation. Various workers have tried to estimate the amount of soil loss due to this faulty cultural practice in this region, viz. Singh and

Singh, 1981, Toky and Ramkrishna, 1981b etc. As high as 146.6 and 179.2 t/ha of soil is lost in first and second year of jhuming under 60-70 per cent land slope (Prasad, *et al.*, 1987). According to another estimate approximately 120 million tonnes of soil volume is being lost each year from the region due to jhuming activity only (Table 8.6). The high amount of average annual rainfall, undulating topography, soil characteristics, faulty land use pattern, pressure from the population explosion, and the increased pace of the developmental activities are the main sources enhancing the pace of erosion of soil specially the top soil, which forms the basis for sustenance of all forms of vegetation. Apart from this, large scale deforestation, mining activities, minor and major land slips and landslides, agriculture on the slopes (other than the shifting cultivation such as Bun method of cultivation, terrace cultivation etc.) are other major contributors to the process of soil erosion and land degradation. Ideally the steep mountain slopes are suitable only for forestry or horticulture and any other type of human intervention is bound to affect the natural balance, but in today's world this situation is next to impossible.

Table 8.6 : Approximate estimated soil loss from Jhuming in NEH Region

State	Jhum Area (ha)	Av. Jhum Cycle (Yr.)	Total soil loss (Million tonnes)
Arunachal Pradesh	35000.0	6	15.2
Assam	22819.0	6	9.9
Manipur	37113.4	10	16.3
Meghalaya	49074.1	5	21.3
Mizoram	35660.4	5	15.5
Nagaland	81153.8	8	35.5
Tripura	16641.8	7	7.3
Total	277462.5		121.0

Source : Mishra, 1999.

The practice of uncontrolled burning of forest biomass is accelerating the pace of environmental pollution and the impact of the same on the climate of the earth is highly dangerous. Therefore, it has become a matter of great scientific and social concern. Thus, the feasibility of prevailing environmental degradation without compromising the natural resources will require efficient and proper management strategies. Apart from the shifting cultivation, the soil and water resources are also threatened by the permanent cultivation on hill slopes. Even the terrace cultivation, which is advocated as the most suitable method of cultivation on hill slopes, in the situation of North-Eastern Himalayan region cannot be considered as very environmentally safe, looking to the rainfall patterns of the region.

Acute Problem of Land Availability for Cultivation and Reduction in Land-Man Ratio

Over hundred of years and in particular in the current century the impact of the human activities on mountain environments has increased considerably. Upland mountainous watersheds are currently habited by more than one-tenth of the world's population. Their environments and livelihoods are threatened by an ever-increasing imbalance between population and the available productive cultivable land. In many places, the activities have already exceeded the carrying capacity of the land, leading to an ever-increasing demand on the land based products. Consequently, the forested upper slopes of the young mountain are being cleared for cultivation, grazing, fodder, fuel wood, and timber. Removal of vegetation on steep slopes, in conjunction with intense monsoon rainfall, is triggering massive erosion and landslides resulting in soil impoverishment and soil loss and deteriorating biophysical environment. This is leading to increasing poverty in mountain communities because the natural resource base of forest, soil, water, plants and animal life on which depends the continued survival of the people of the mountainous region is decreasing at an alarming rate. Measures to control the degradation are required before the ecological balance is irreversibly damaged.

Due to decreased land-man ratio, at present not more than 5 per cent land in Arunachal Pradesh, Meghalaya, Manipur, Mizoram and Nagaland and about 30 per cent in Tripura and Assam are available for cultivation which is a sensitivity factor supporting a large population on land. Interestingly, it is found that areas with adverse man-cultivable land ratio (e.g., Mizoram, Meghalaya and Nagaland) are also registering highest growth rate in population. If the present trend in population growth is not checked, this would result into a serious problem on available land and also upset the ecological balance as more forest area would be needed to be cleared to settle down the growing population and to fulfil the needs of increasing population. The recent human interventions have given rise to disturbing impact on the mountain environments. Large scale changes occurring in the mountain environment have resulted in widespread human miseries. The impact of such changes is not restricted only to the mountain areas but have also led to socio-economic impacts on plains. Because of the deterioration of the mountain environment as well as the urgent need to ensure sustainable habitat, national and international institutional have made the mountain environment a matter of increasing concern.

Sustainability of Different Land Use Systems of the Region

Soils of the North Eastern Himalayan Region fall under Class VI to Class VIII as per the Land Use Capability Classification. According to this classification, lands falling in above four categories are not suitable for cultivation. Therefore, the hill slopes should not at all be exposed to any type of erosive activities or by putting the same under cultivation. The processes of shifting cultivation and for that matter any type of disturbance to the natural system is bound to adversely affect the natural balance of the system. In the established terraced system also, there are huge losses of the soil that is evident from Table 8.7, that shows the sediment transportation rate of some tributaries of the river Brahmaputra.

The various socio-economic constraints in our country force the poor tribal farmers (mainly subsistence farmers) to practice the cultivation on steepest hill slopes either in the form of shifting or settled type of farming for their survival. They are wholly dependent on the forest resources and shifting cultivation has acquired the form of the way of living. The indiscriminate and haphazard developmental activities, road side erosion, minor land slides etc. are other factors contributing for the speedy deterioration of the health of the hills. River meandering, widening of the mouths of active gullies, deepening of the gullies in the steep terrain and cutting and washing off of the river banks are several other factors causing erosion on hills and devastating floods in valley region.

Table 8.7: Sediment production rates in Brahmaputra river basin in North-East India

Rivers	Sediment Production Rate (t/ha/yr)
Brahmaputra (Pandu)	8.04
Northern Tributaries	
Jia-bharali	47.21
Puthimari	28.87
Buriari	24.06
Pagladia	18.83
Manas	15.81
Subansiri	9.59
Southern Tributaries	
Dibang	37.65
Lohit	19.60
Burhidihang	11.29
Desang	6.22
Dhansiri (South)	3.79
Kopili	2.30

Source : Anonymous, 1991.

Strategies for Natural Resources Management for Sustainable Development of North-East India

Managing the mountain environment is a complex task due to their specific characteristics. Notwithstanding the contribution these can make, the concepts and methods of natural resources management for mountain environment are in a rudimentary, evolving stage. Serious, analytical and integrative contributions are needed to strengthen these vital areas. Accordingly, natural resources management in mountain environment cannot at present be a fully perspective guide to human activities. It is the accumulation of knowledge from various similar situations and then several resource management strategies that will provide a more comprehensive perspective tool for the future. One of the major challenges for integrated mountain development or upland mountain watershed management is to ensure that the needs and aspirations of the people are suitably matched without compromising the ability of future generations to meet their own needs. A comprehensive strategy for natural resources management in mountainous/hilly areas might, therefore, be based on holistic and interdisciplinary understanding of both the societies and habitat with a dynamic framework. For agriculture on steep slopes, contour bunds, bench terraces or a combination of both measures help in reducing soil and water losses to a minimum permissible limit. Vertical intervals of these measures need to be kept within a limit of 0.5 to 1.0 m for operational convenience. These measures can be constructed with the use of locally available materials and resources.

The various approaches followed in the past to replace *jhuming* have drastically failed mainly due to the fact that they were some types of impositions on the *jhumias*. It is however learnt from the experience that the *jhuming* cannot be replaced from the region. Micro-watershed based farming systems with different farming systems components has acquired a socio-cultural and religious nature. More so, the poor sustenance farmers would need economically strong and viable alternatives to shift from their age-old practice to a more settled form of cultivation of steep hill slopes. The farmers of Jaintia hills have abandoned this practice as they have coal and limestone deposits in their lands that are more remunerative than any form of cultivation. Alternative farming systems approach as developed by the ICAR, such as agriculture, horticulture, agri-horti-silvi-pastoral, livestock based etc., should be popularized so that the farmer's need should be fulfilled as well as the resource should also be conserved for further utilization. These watershed based farming systems help in conservation of soil and water and are more remunerative. The mixed farming component of shifting cultivation should also be incorporated in watershed based farming systems.

Ensuring People's Participation in Natural Resources Conservation and Management

The immediate task before us is to make strategies using the scientific know-how available with us to preserve, protect conserve and efficiently utilize our precious natural resources to boost the economy of the region with sustainability of the resources. In this process the most degrading practice of shifting cultivation will be required to be suitably modified if not completely stopped, which has already harmed the health of the environment and ecology immensely by resources depletion. The tribal mentality needs to be changed completely by demonstrating them the ill effects of their existing cultivation practice and by providing them more remunerative technological packages in return. Promotion of afforestation programmes on denuded hill slopes and waste lands is the need of the hour as well as the judicious utilization of land and water resources as per land capability classification and availability respectively, would not only ensure higher productivity but also improve the economy of the region with resources sustainability. As no effort is successful till the actual beneficiaries have active participation in implementing any programme. The education of the general public is a must so that they should fully realize that the ill done today by them will be a curse for their coming generations. The soil and water conservation programmes for integrated watershed management, therefore, must be such that the farmers of the region should be involved completely. Other erosive factors should also be completely checked in the hills and mountainous region so as to avoid catastrophes in the valley regions too.

Participatory Integrated Watershed Management Approach

In order to achieve the developmental objectives sustainability, it is a must to restore the degraded hill ecosystem with proper and efficient management of land and water resources. Strategies for ascertaining the relentless destruction of sustainable livelihood particularly afflicting indigenous and tribal people and the resource management strategies for sustainable development of north-eastern hill ecosystem include: quantitative and qualitative assessment of spatial and temporal distribution, to intercept and absorb the kinetic energy of falling rain drops (by increasing the forest cover for checking the erosion potential), reducing the erosive velocity of water on the steep slopes by increasing the vegetal cover, to induce and enhance the infiltration in the soil, application of water conservation methods, water harvesting in built up structures, following *in situ* water conservation techniques, reduction of evaporation from open water surfaces, checking the seepage losses from the wetted surfaces. Apart from this, efficient utilization of water for crop production also needs to be practiced. All these should be popularized on watersheds and repeated observations of soil, water and nutrient losses should also be taken to ascertain the positive effects of integrated watershed management principles. As the topsoil is the only productive layer, there is an immediate requirement to conserve the topsoil. The soil resources management strategy include: land use surveys and mapping of various soil types of the region; possibly by the remote sensing satellites, identification of waste and degraded lands, landslide prone zones and mining areas, permitting agricultural operations as per the classification of agricultural lands, minimizing the area under shifting cultivation, adoption of various agronomic and engineering techniques for checking the soil erosion, drainage line treatment, plugging the active gullies, restricting the heavy earth moving and erosion causing activities especially prior and during monsoon season, and practice of soil conservation measures with minimum disturbance of surface cover. For this purpose various soil conservation measures, such as engineering structures (like bench terraces, contour bunding, half moon terraces, grassed water ways etc.) and agronomic measures (like sodding, vegetative barriers, strip cropping, avoiding the growing of erosion permitting crops like maize on steep hill slopes, permitting the growth of natural vegetal covers to check the erosive velocity of flowing water and preventing associated soil and nutrient loss due to erosion are required to be adopted. By following the above proper management strategies, not only the capacity of land and water resources can be harnessed to their fullest extent but also the resources can be sustained for long for the benefit of future generations. The worldwide efforts to control and check the soil erosion from steep hill slopes show that these measures have been found to check the land degradation by retaining 80-100 per cent of annual rainfall *in situ*, contributing towards ground water recharge. People's participation is a must for success of the system.

Strengthening the Indigenous Systems of Resources (Land, Water and Ecologic) Management

Some of the indigenous techniques for land and water management developed traditionally in the region are the *Zabo* system of terrace farming in Nagaland (Gokhle *et al,* 1985; Prasad and Sharma, 1994), *Bench terracing* cultivation in Sikkim and *Panikheti* in Nagaland (Gokhle *et al.*, 1984), *Bamboo drip* irrigation system of Jowai in Meghalaya (Singh, 1989), and sustainable land and water management system of *Apatanis* in Arunachal Prdesh (Chaudhary *et al.*, 1990). There is a need to suitably modify these techniques for individual agro-climatic conditions and to spread the good features of these systems in other parts of the region too.

Conclusions

The North-Eastern Himalayan Region is experiencing the most serious problem of worsening poverty and degradation of natural resources. There is a great deal of concern for conservation of natural resources, which are the basis of human sustenance. Though the region has been endowed with ample potential of all kinds yet the development rate is very poor consequently the backwardness in all spheres of human interest. The resources base and environmental conditions of the region offer vast opportunities for resource base intensification with conservation. The need for making the development more effective and sustainable in mountainous region thus, warrants us to adopt a comprehensive land and water use policy, exploitation of mountain flora and forest, underground mineral resources etc. based on scientific principles and planned management on watershed basis and with active participation of the people of the region and frequent monitoring of the whole range of the mountain natural resources. Integrated development approach is considered the best for natural resource management, environmental protection and overall well-being of the hill people as it takes into account numerous interrelated factors into consideration. In fact, this should be a policy approach in developmental planning approach of natural resources conservation and management.

REFERENCES

Anonymous, 1985. *Report of the Working Group on Development of North East Council,* Shillong, pp. 83-84.

Anonymous, 1985. *Technological Bull. I — Crop Science of ICAR Res. Complex for NEH Region during the decade* (1975-1984).

Anonymous, 1992. *Census of India 1991.* Series - 1, Paper - 2 of 1992.

Anonymous, 1995. *Basic Statistics of North Eastern Region 1995.* North Eastern Council, Ministry of Home Affairs, Government of India, Shillong.

Anonymous, 1991 *Annual Mayhem in Assam.* In: Floods, and environmental myths. State of India's Environment: A citizen's report., CSE, Ahmedabad.

Anonymous, 1997. Geographical area, recorded and actual forest cover in NEH region of India. *The Hindu Survey of the Environment* (Tables).

Anonymous, 1997. *The Hindu Survey of Environment, 1997,* Madras.

Basu, D.N. and Guha, G.S., 1996. *Agroclimatic Regional Planning in India.* Concept Pub. Co., New Delhi.

Bisht, B.S. and Tiwari, P.C., 1996. Land use planning for sustainable resources development in Kumaon Lesser Himalaya — a case study of Gomti watershed. *Int. J. Sustain. Dev. World Ecol.* 3 : 23-34.

Black, John, 1969. Some environmental concerns, as quoted In: Monteith, J.L. (1990). *Can Sustainability be Questioned.* Proc. of the Int. Sympo. on Natural Resources Management for Sustainable Agriculture. 6-10 Feb., 1990, New Delhi.

Borthakur, B.C. 1998. Sustainability in crop production: The Challenges in NE India. *National seminar on Management Strategies for North Eastern Hilly Ecosystem,* ICAR Research Complex for NEH Region, Umiam 8-10th August, ABSTRACTS, p. 57.

Chaudhary, R.G.; Dwivedi, R.N.; Prasad, R.N. and Dutta, K.K (1990). Research needs for land and water management for enhancing agricultural production in Arunachal Pradesh. Proceedings of the workshop on research needs on land and water management for enhancing agricultural production in Eastern region W.T.C. for Eastern Region, Bhubaneshwar, Orissa, India, 93-120.

Gokhle, A.M., Talitsuba, Kevichusa R., Angami, T. and Bendangnungsang, S. (1984). *Panikheti on Mountain slopes - Picture Essay.* State Council of Education Research & Training, Government of Nagaland, Kohima.

Gokhle, A.M.; Zeliang, D.K.; Kevichusa, R.; Angami, T. and Bendangnungsang, S. (1985). *The Use of Alder Trees.* State Council of Education Research & Training, Education Department, Government of Nagaland, Kohima.

Goldsmith, E.; Hilgard, N.; Bunyard, P. and McCully, P., (1990). *5000 Days to save the Planet.* Paul Hamlyn Publishing Co. London.

Hazarika, R.N. *Options for the long term management of water resources in the Brahmaputra basin.* Souvenir, 2nd water resources day celebration organizing committee (1998).

Lal, B., 1998. Sustainable resources management for soil and water conservation on hill ecosystem. *National Seminar on Management Strategies for North Eastern Hilly Ecosystem,* ICAR Research Complex for NEH Region, Umiam 8-10th August, ABSTRACTS, p. 20.

Mahajan, V.S., 1987. Population and Agriculture in North Eastern Economy. In *Patterns of North Eastern Economy.* Deep and Deep Pub., New Delhi, 96-105.

Mishra, A. K., 1998. Identification of Water Scarcity Periods for Crop Planning at Umiam Farm. *National Seminar on Management Strategies for North Eastern Hilly Ecosystem,* ICAR Research Complex for NEH Region, Umiam, 8-10 August, ABSTRACTS, p. 22.

Mishra, A.K., 1998. An inventory of some potential renewable energy resources of North East India. *Seminar on Renewable Energy Resources Development,* 5th June, 1998. North East India Council of Social Science Research, Shillong.

Mishra, A.K.; Singh, R.K.P.; Aggarwal, K.N. and Gupta, S.K., 1998. An inventory of some potential renewable energy resources of NEH India. *Agril. Engg. Today.* 22(3-4): 17-27.

Mishra, A.K., 1999. *An Approximation of Soil Loss in Jhuming in North Eastern Region of India.* ICAR Res. Complex for NEH Region, Barapani, Meghalaya, India (Unpub.).

Mishra, A.K., 1998, *An estimation of environmental pollution due to burning of forest biomass in shifting cultivation.* Unpub.

Mishra, A.K. and Gupta, S.K., 1998. Land and Water resources management strategies for sustainable development of North Eastern Hill Ecosystem. *National Seminar on Management Strategies for North Eastern Hilly Ecosystem,* ICAR Research Complex for NEH Region, Umiam 8-10th August, ABSTRACTS, p. 25.

Prasad, R.N.; Pati Ram; Barua, R.C.; and Munna Ram, 1981. Soil fertility management in NEH region. *Res. Bull. No. 9.* ICAR Res. Complex for NEH Region, Barapani, Meghalaya, India.

Prasad, R.N.; Singh, A. and Varma, A., 1987. *Application of research findings for management of land and water resources in Eastern Himalayan Region.* ICAR Research Complex for NEH Region, Barapani, Meghalaya, India.

Prasad, R.N. and Sharma, U.C., 1990. Shifting Cultivation NEH Region — Problems and Solutions. *Newsline* (Weekly) October 19-26. Shillong, Meghalaya.

Prasad, R.N. and Sharma, U.C. (1994). *Potential Indigenous Farming Systems of North Eastern Hill region.* ICAR Research Complex for N.E.H. Region, Umroi Road, Barapani, Meghalaya.

Rambabu, Tejwani, K.G.; Aggarwal, M.C. and Chandra, S., 1978. Rainfall erosion potential and isoerodent map of India. *Bull. No. 2* CSWCRTI, Dehradun.

Ramkrishna, P.S., 1990. Agricultural systems of the North Eastern Hill Region of India. In Agroecology: Researching the ecological basis for sustainable agriculture. Stephen, R. Gliessman (ed.). *Ecological Series 78.* Springer Verlag Inc. New York : 251-274.

Sharma, U.C. and Mishra, A.K., 1998. Deforestation in North Eastern region of India and traditional wisdom in range management for resources and environmental conservation. *Paper in the International Symp. on Agro-environmental Issues and Future Strategies : Towards 21st Century.* May 25-30, 1998, University of Agriculture, Faisalabad, Pakistan.

Sharma, U.C., 1996. Uttar Poorva Ke Jal Sansadhan va Unka Prabandh *Poorvottar*

Parvatiya Krishi, ICAR Research Complex for NEH Region, Umiam, 3: 1-7.

Sharma, U.C. and Sarma, B.K. (ed.), 1991. ICAR Research Complex for North Eastern Hill region — Actions and Achievements. *National Seminar on Resources Management for Hill Agriculture,* ICAR Research Complex for NEH region, Barapani, 28-30 Oct. 1991. Souvenir : 1-27.

Singh, A. (1989). *Bamboo Drip Irrigation System.* ICAR Research Complex for N.E.H. Region, Umroi Road, Barapani, Meghalaya.

Singh, A. and Singh, M.D., 1981. Soil erosion hazards in North-Eastern Hill region, *Research Bull.* No. 10, Div. of Agril. Engg., ICAR Research Complex for NEH Region, Umiam, Meghalaya.

Singh, D.K. 1998. Soil and water conservation for sustainable hill agriculture—the management strategies for the north-eastern hill ecosystem. *National Seminar on Management Strategies for North Eastern Hilly Ecosystem,* ICAR Research Complex for NEH Region, Umiam, 8-10th August, ABSTRACTS p. 17.

Toky, O.P. and Ramkrishna, P.S., 1981b. Runoff and infiltration losses related to shifting agriculture (Jhum) in North Eastern India. *Environmental Conservation. 8:* 313-321.

9

NORTH-EAST STATES : Considerations for Determining Priorities in Social Science Research

T. B. Lahiri

N.E. Offers Multiple Choices

North-Eastern Region of India offers an unique opportunity for Social Scientists. If there is a desire to study human diversity, to explore human adjustments with ecological conditions of multiple variety, to gauge the impact of the recurrent natural hazards (primarily floods) on human settlements, human outlook associated with inaccessibility and isolation, retreating natural resources under pressure of population, problem of social communication and integration in the presence of scores of dialects specially in tribal areas, long and difficult terrain of its international boundaries coupled with cross-border activities affecting indigenous demographic structure and peace, politics of militancy and terrorist activities, no other region in India than N.E. could provide so many choices for research by social scientists, each one being significant. But in no case, if the objective is to bring out the truth and truth alone, the path is not going to be easy. Indeed, the road is hazardous and risky but the travel carries with it the potential of finding new realities which may help in visualising right courses for bringing harmony and fostering integrated development.

I. PRESENT SCENARIO : BRIEF REVIEW

Geopolitical Frame

In Assam, there is a long history of alienation between plains people and

Table 9.1 : N.E. States: Certain Basic Data

	State	Date of statehood/ Present Territorial Limits *	Rank in N.E. by Area	Rank in N.E. by Population size (1991)	Rank in N.E. by Literacy % (1993)	Rank in N.E. by Two Community Facilities	
						Drinking Water supply % of Villages covered	Rural Electrification % of Villages covered (1998-99)
1.	Arunachal Pradesh	1972	1	6	7 (41.59)	2 (46.5)	6 (56.0)
2.	Assam	1987	2	1	6 (52.89)	6 (28.4)	2 (97.0)
3.	Nagaland	1972	6	5	2 (61.65)	3 (41.6)	1 (98.8)
4.	Manipur	1972	4	3	4 (59.89)	4 (40.4)	3 (80.0)
5.	Mizoram	1987	5	7	1 (82.27)	1 (70.3)	5 (56.0)
6.	Meghalaya	1972	3	4	5 (49.10)	5 (40.3)	5 (47.0)
7.	Tripura	1972	7	2	3 (60.44)	N.A.	4 (64.1)

*Except Assam, other states of N.E. were Union Territories before given statehood.

hill tribes. Government of India set up several commissions/committees for resolving the issues related to grievances of hill people and their demand for autonomy. Of these commissions and committees, special mention may be made of Pataskar Commission (1964) and Ashok Mehta Committee (1967). Through series of discussions between Government and APHLC and other groups punctuated by violence and stormy agitations eventually the present political organisation of the N.E. states has emerged (Table 9.1). In place of Assam, there is now 7 sister states, by area, barring Sikkim and Goa (smallest), the tiny states of the N.E. occupy the lowest ranks, viz., Meghalaya, Manipur, Mizoram, Nagaland and Tripura (in descending order).

In spite of states' reorganisation, geo-political unrest is far from over. ULFA's (United Liberation Front of Assam) separatist aspirations, Bodo demand for autonomy, insurgency in Manipur and Nagaland, specially Kachin trouble-zone of Manipur and tension between Brahmaputra Valley and Barak Valley people are still absorbing much of nation's resources in fire-fighting. It is a regret that post-independent India has by and large deviated from the path of non-violent demonstrations for political objectives. The militancy and insurgency in N.E. find some support unfortunately enough, from neighbouring foreign countries. Arunachal shares borders with China and Bhutan ; Assam with Bhutan; Nagaland, Manipur and Mizoram with Myanmar; Meghalaya and Tripura with Bangladesh.

Demographic Profile

N.E. states together has an area of 255,028 sq.km. that is about 8 per cent of India's area which is the home of nearly 4 per cent of India's population with an average density of 123 per sq.km. against India's average of 267 (1991) (Table 9.2).

The population distribution, mainly for physiographic reasons, is very uneven. Arunachal the largest State in N.E. supports the lowest share of population. But Tripura the smallest state, is only second to Assam in pupulation percentage. However, Assam is the giant holding about 71 per cent of the regional population. Naturally, density of population is highest in Assam, Tripura and lowest in Arunachal.

Population growth-rate (1981-91) except Assam, is higher in all states than India Average with Nagaland at top (Table 9.3). Assam's growth-rate is almost same as India's.

In another aspect, Assam differs from rest of N.E. states, i.e. low

Table 9.2 : N.E. India : Salient Demographic Features of States *vis-a-vis* India, 1991

States	Area Sq.Km.	State's Area as % of N.E.	State's Area as % of India	Population	State's Popn. as % of N.E. India	State's Popn. as % of N.E. India	Density per Sq. Km.	State's Rural SC Popn. as % of State's R.P.	State's Rural ST Popn. as % of State's R.P.
1. Arunachal Pradesh	83,578	32.79	3.29	858,392	2.73	0.10	10	0.4	68.7
2. Assam	78,523	30.80	2.38	22,294,562	71.05	2.63	284	7.2	13.9
3. Manipur	22,356	8.76	0.67	1,826,714	5.81	0.21	82	1.3	43.5
4. Meghalaya	22,489	8.81	0.68	1,760,626	5.60	0.20	78	0.3	90.8
5. Mizoram	21,078	8.26	0.64	686,217	2.18	0.08	33	0.1	96.3
6. Nagaland	16,527	6.48	0.50	1,215,573	3.87	0.14	73	0.08	93.2
7. Tripura	10,477	4.10	0.31	2,744,827	8.76	0.31	262	8.4	35.9
Total of N.E. States	255,028	100.00	8.47	31,386,911	100.00	3.69	123		

percentage of tribal population among total rural population of the state (13.9). Mizoram has the highest concentration of tribal population (96.3). It is interesting that though Arunachal is mainly a hilly forested state, there is a sizeable non-tribal population (Table 9.2).

There are about 55 tribes living in N.E. states. They are in some cases divided into sub-groups. Works of Verrier Elwin on NEFA (Arunachal), K.P. Chattopadhyay's *Khasi Kinship and Social Organisation*, D.N. Mazumdar's *The Garo and other ethnographers* studies on sociology of kinship throw light on tribal organisations and behavioural pattern. Sociologists and anthropologists have studied politics at village level or community power structures. Such findings are significant for promotion of broad-based fraternity.

Use of multiple languages and dialects convey cultural heterogeneity of the N.E. region. For example, in Nagaland, in addition to English, Ao, Konyak, Angami, Sumi and Lotha languages are used by respective tribe. Similarly, in Arunachal, various tribes like Monpa, Aka, Miji Nishi, Apatami, Hill Miri, Adi, Idu etc. have their own languages. However adoption of Roman script under the influence of the church specially in Mizoram and Meghalaya has made communication relatively easier. Assam has a large Bengali speaking population particularly in Barak Valley. In Tripura too, Bengali is the chief medium though even in that small state, two other languages are in use, viz., Kokbarak and Manipuri. In Manipur, in spite of large presence of Nagas and Kukis, using their respective languages, Manipuri is the chief language of the state and has won national recognition. Manipuri folk art, music and dance have wider appeal much beyond the borders of the N.E. region.

Perhaps urbanisation could be a vehicle for cultural-mix. But except Nagaland and Manipur, the rate of urbanisation is much lower than national average in rest of the states. Interestingly, Assam has the lowest percentage of population living in urban areas (Table 9.3).

State of Economy

In all the hill states of the N.E. participation ratio (workers as percentage of total population) is higher than national average. Possibly it is a reflection of subsistence type of economy. In Assam and Tripura, participation rate is lower than national average.

In all the states, agriculture and allied activities is the chief source of living. The percentage of agricultural workers among main workers being

Table 9.3 : Relative Development Index with some selected criteria *vis-a-vis* India, 1993

(Figures within brackets indicate All India Average)

	State	Relative Dev. Index	Popn. Growth Rate per year	Urbanisation %	Literacy %	Female Literacy %	Workers as % of Total Popn.	Agri. & allied workers as % of main workers	Per Capita Foodgrains Production Kgs.	Road length per 100 Sq. Km.	Per Capita Bank Credit
1.	Arunachal Pradesh	66	3.11	12.80	41.59	29.69	46.24	67.26	210	8.51	320
		(100)	(2.14)	(25.73)	(52.21)	(39.29)	(37.46)	(66.92)	(173)	(60.14)	(1978)
2.	Assam	54	2.13	11.10	52.89	43.03	36.09	73.50	119	81.98	581
		(100)	(2.14)	(25.73)	(52.21)	(39.29)	(37.46)	(66.92)	(173)	(60.14)	(1978)
3.	Manipur	55	2.54	27.52	59.89	47.60	42.18	69.97	151	29.43	483
		(100)	(2.14)	(25.73)	(52.21)	(39.29)	(37.46)	(66.92)	(173)	(60.14)	(1978)
4.	Meghalaya	54	2.80	18.60	49.10	44.85	42.67	74.21	75	28.59	435
		(100)	(2.14)	(25.73)	(52.21)	(39.29)	(37.46)	(66.92)	(173)	(60.14)	(1978)
5.	Mizoram	54	3.35	46.10	82.27	78.60	48.91	65.77	82	15.50	343
		(100)	(2.14)	(25.73)	(52.21)	(39.29)	(37.46)	(66.92)	(173)	(60.14)	(1978)
6.	Nagaland	55	4.60	17.21	61.65	54.75	42.68	75.20	93	47.59	807
		(100)	(2.14)	(25.73)	(52.21)	(39.29)	(37.46)	(66.92)	(173)	(60.14)	(1978)
7.	Tripura	55	2.95	15.30	60.44	49.65	31.14	63.79	156	16.47	714
		(100)	(2.14)	(25.73)	(52.21)	(39.29)	(37.46)	(66.92)	(173)	(60.14)	(1978)

Source : 'Profile of Districts', November 1993, Published by Centre for Monitoring Indian Economy Pvt. Ltd., Bombay.

Table 9.4 : N.E. States : Land-use Pattern, 1990 (Satellite based data)

	State	Argicultural Land as % of total area			Plantation	Forest	Wasteland
		Kharif	Rabi	Double-cropped			
1.	Arunachal Pradesh	(a) 4.55% (b) 2.46%	—	—	—	82.81%	—
2.	Assam	37.61%	22.22%	18.93%	12.34%	21.90%	13.50%
3.	Nagaland	(a) 28.58% (b) 2.35%	— —	—	—	68.09%	—
4.	Manipur	(a) 25.91% (b) 7.58%	—	—	—	63.33%	—
5.	Mizoram	(a) 4.06% (b) 3.26%	—	—	—	92.81%	
6.	Meghalaya	(a) 32.56%	—	—	—	63.80%	—
7.	Tripura	(a) 4.81% (b) 14.76% (c) 4.48%	—	—	—	36.90%	—

(a) Under shifting cultivation.
(b) Under settled agriculture.

(c) Double-cropped area.

Source :National Remote Sensing Agency, Hyderabad.

higher than national average or almost at par with it, i.e. Tripura and Mizoram (Table 9.3). But agricultural productivity as measured through per capita foodgrains production, is much lower than national average with the sole exception of Arunachal. Meghalaya is at the bottom (Table 9.3).

Though agriculture is the chief occupation, land under cultivation is not extensive except Assam (Table 9.4) But what is alarming is that still in all the hill states shifting cultivation (*Jhum*) remained the dominant practice. Permanent agricultural land in hill states of the N.E. is very limited. Assam is the solitary exception with Tripura a poor second.

Naturally, practice of shifting cultivation is taking a heavy toll of the rich forest resources of the N.E. In spite of active afforestation programme, substantial decline in forest area is evident in all the states except for a small gain in Nagaland and Tripura (Table 9.5). Deforestation is an important contributing factor for rapid soil erosion, increasing frequency of floods and decreasing agricultural productivity.

Agricultural diversification and double-cropping are practically absent except Assam. Thanks to tea plantation there is a sizeable commercial cultivation in Assam covering about 12.34 per cent of the land in the state (Table 9.4). Nearly 52 per cent of tea-garden area of India is located in Assam.

Table 9.5 : N.E. States : Change in Forest Area from 1991 to 1993 (Sq.Km.)

State	Lose due to *Jhuming*	Other Reasons	Total Loss	Gain due to Afforestation	Net Loss/ Gain
1. Arunachal Pradesh	70	28	98	—	−98
2. Assam	165	190	355	112	−243
3. Manipur	28	36	64	—	−64
4. Meghalaya	110	2	112	6	−106
5. Mizoram	256	—	256	100	−156
6. Nagaland	63	—	63	90	+27
7. Tripura	10	27	37	40	+3
Total	702	281	983	348	−633

Source : Forest Survey, Ministry of Environment & Forest, Dehra Dun, Government of India, 1993.

Physical Constraints

If the actual rainfall in a year of an area exceeds normal rainfall by more than twice the mean deviation, that is a flood year. It is almost an annual feature in the Brahmaputra Valley; worst affected part is the Nalbari Sub-Division of Kamrup district of Assam. Floods severely damage surface transport facilities and is a serious hindrance for development.

In all hilly N.E. states accessibility is very poor. By the standard of road length per 100 sq.km., achievement so far in all states fall far short of national average. Exceptions are Tripura ranking first followed by Assam (Table 9.3).

Overall Relative Development Index of the States

Overall relative development index determined by the Centre for Monitoring Indian Economy Pvt. Ltd., Bombay, as evident by performance against 32 selected criteria, is by and large accepted in the country. RDIs of states in the N.E. showing position against certain key indicators is presented in Table 9.3.

Surprisingly by RDI, Arunachal is slightly up the ladder. In respect of the other states, difference is very marginal. Though individual indicators show sharp differences. In literacy, Mizoram is outstanding followed by Nagaland. In road communication, Tripura and Assam outshine others. In per captia bank credit, Nagaland tops the list perhaps due to growth of tiny sector (Table 9.3). By rural electrification too, Nagaland stands highest but that position is taken by Mizoram when percentage of villages covered by drinking water supply is considered (Table 9.1). Not withstanding, such differences about individual criteria, plus and minuses when all 32 criteria are considered, result is more or less same RDI for all constituent states of the N.E. In other words, every unit of the N.E. states is backward and will continue to require special support.

II. POSSIBLE PRIORITIES IN SOCIAL SCIENCE RESEARCH

Endeavour has been made to present salient characteristics of the present north-eastern scenario which may guide in determining possible priorities of social science research.

It appears, research which will show the way for fostering amity and accord between different ethnic groups in highly heterogeneous habitat of the N.E. should draw foremost attention. Development has not been able to take driver's seat because of militancy, insurgency and terrorist activities. It is high time to throw light on suicidal nexus between political elements who failed to capture power and patronage of violent activities. More and more deployment of army is not the answer. The urge for peace is inherent in human beings. People will have to be made aware of the forces that threaten basic condition needed for forward march. They themselves would organize defence against evil forces once social scientists boldly and convincingly expose them through selected case studies.

Fast rate of population growth should be a matter of great concern. Whether there is a relationship between faith and failure of family planning programmes specially in hill states is to be examined. Unlike Kerala's, high literacy rate among hill people has still no bearing on population growth rate.

Linguistic extra loyalties which at times create social barriers and threaten linguistic minorities in the region could be curbed by providing instances of simultaneous flowering through symbiotic examples, of which are available elsewhere in the world.

Destruction of the most important natural resource of the region i.e., forests through widespread shifting cultivation should be prevented. Beginning has been made through terracing, contour-bunding etc. But still a long way to go.

Promotion of tiny sector, i.e. rural industries seems to have a distinct possibility in view of available human skill and large-scale electrification.

Lack of accessibility is a front which calls for national attention. Social scientists may, through case studies, show positive relationship between higher accessibility and better growth, how better communication (in broad terms) may wipe out unnecessary fear, reliance on dumb signs and a kind of helplessness that erodes human strength and creativity. It is understood that such instances exist in corners of the north-east. Could we foster it?

There must be some other vital areas of concern which remained left out here. It is trusted that such gaps would be filled up fruitfully by others.

REFERENCES

CMIE, Bombay : *Profile of Districts,* 1993.

Government of India, National Remote Sensing Agencies, Hyderabad : *Satellite Based Data*, 1990.

Govt. of India : *Census of India Reports*, 1991.

ICSSR, New Delhi : *A Survey of Research in Geography*, Popular Prakashan, Bombay, 1972.

ICSSR, New Delhi : *A Survey of Research in Sociology and Social Anthropology,* Popular Prakashan, Bombay, 1974.

Ministry of Environment, Government of India, Dehra Dun : *Forest Survey*, 1993.

NIRD, Hyderabad : *Census of India Reports*, 1991.

Publications Division, Government of India : *The Gazetteer of India,* Vol. 1, Country & People, 1973.

10

FORMATION OF THE APPROPRIATE DEVELOPMENT PARADIGM OF NORTH-EAST INDIA

N. N. Bhattacharyya

North-East India, is located between 22°N and 29°N latitudes and 89°46'E and 97°30'E longitudes and covers an area of 2,55,000 sq. km which supports a population of about 32 million. The region borders with China, Bhutan, Myanmar and Bangladesh and hence it occupies an extremely strategic position. It is connected with the mainland by a narrow corridor of foothill land in North Bengal. This link is also subjected to occasional disruptions due to heavy rain and floods. Such location and terrain conditions like Tertiary mountains and hills, Archean plateaus, river valleys and mountain basins make it an isolated region. The climate of the region may be identified as tropical monsoon with local variations. The terrain conditions, soil types, rainfall, humidity and temperature conditions of the region support an altitudinally distributed vegetations which provide habitats and niches for different types of herbivores and their predators, birds, insects, reptiles and fishes. The region is endowed with a variety of minerals like petroleum, coal, limestone, sillimanite and a large reservoir of hydel power potential.

According to 1991 census, out of 31.55 million persons of the region as many as 27 million persons lived in 44,531 villages and the rest representing 21.23 per cent of the population inhabited 183 urban centres including 8 cities. Thus India's North-East is one of the most unurbanized regions of India. There are wide variations in the distribution of population and settlement within North-East India. The mountains and hills of the region support hill tribals with their sparse settlements. The plain tribals, tea garden workers and large number of Nepali settlers are found to live in the foothills while the interfluves of the major river valleys are inhabited mainly by non-tribal population.

It is to be mentioned that barring Assam most of the states of the region are late comers to the process of development as they were created subsequent to the first decade of planning. The Naga Hills district of Assam and the Tuensang area of NEFA were separated for the formation of Nagaland in 1957 in the wake of insurgency there and it was elevated to a full state in 1963. After conceding Nagaland it was very difficult to keep the other hill areas of Assam from getting their respective state. Meghalaya was formed with two hill districts, namely Garo Hills and United Khasi and Jayantia Hills of Assam on April 2, 1970. Under the North Eastern Reorganisation Act of 1971, Meghalaya was granted full statehood along with Manipur and Tripura, Arunachal Pradesh and Mizoram were made Union Territories and the last two units also gained full statehood in February 1987.

Different geographical, economic and social factors have contributed substantially to the emergence of a centripetal force among the traditional inhabitants of India's North-East. The whole North-East India became a melting pot for various ethnolinguistic groups like Austro-Asiatic, Tibeto-Chinese, Aryan etc. and a type of Mongoloid culture has been created in the region. But due to imposition of various social, economic and political forces compounded by linguistic and political gulf existing between different groups of people, the centripetal force has now become weakened in the policy of North-East India. The current trouble in the region is due to geographic isolation, long years of neglect and sudden exposure of relatively backward societies to the complexities of modern system imposed by the Government of India.

Barring Assam, Manipur and Tripura, the majority of the population is tribal ranging from 79 per cent in Arunachal, 80 per cent in Meghalaya, 89 per cent in Nagaland to 94 per cent in Mizoram. The general density of population in these tribal states is low, infrastructure weak and technology primitive. The tribal people of the whole region including hills of Assam, Manipur and Tripura have developed different techniques of their own hunting, fishing, agriculture, house pattern, bridge construction etc. which were adjusted to the ecosystem and guided by tribal belief. In their area man-nature relationship was always congenial and mutually beneficial. But as change is inevitable, the tribals are directly exposed to sophisticated world from their slumber giving very less time to tune themselves with the new ones. Such sudden exposure to the new world has created more harm to man-nature relationship.

The economic structure of the states of North-East India is dominated by agriculture and allied activities. But the land under cultivation in the region is only 16 per cent of its total geographical area. It varies from 2.5 per cent in Arunachal Pradesh to 7.2 per cent in Manipur, 9.4 per cent in Meghalaya, 4 per cent in Mizoram, 15 per cent in Nagaland, 36 per cent in Tripura and 45 per cent in Assam. The shifting cultivation is the common mode of agriculture in the hilly areas. It is practised by about 4,44,000 families over an area of 3,900 sq. km. This method of cultivation has given rise to problems of land-slide and erosion, deforestation, loss of fertility of the soil etc. Flood, bank erosion and drought in certain areas are the main hurdles to the development of agriculture in the plains. Besides, there is little crop diversification in the states of North-East India. About 76 per cent of cultivated area is under foodgrains, 5 per cent under oil seeds and 3 per cent under fibre crops. The foodgrain situation in the region is not good. The requirement of foodgrain in the year 1994-95 was 6.708 million tonnes which would rise to 7.940 million tonnes in 2000-2001, while its production is likely to be only 6.346 million tonnes during 2000-2001 (ICAR estimates). Various institutions like Assam Agricultural University at Jorhat, Fishery College at Raha, Veterinary College at Khanapara, Guwahati, Fishery College in Tripura, Veterinary College in Mizoram, Home Science College in Tura, Horticulture College in Arunachal Pradesh etc. are coming up which should strengthen the agricultural infrastructure in the region. Perhaps the transfer of technology has emerged the biggest constraint in increasing agricultural productivity of the entire region. All these show the need of scientific land management for extension of agriculture in the region.

The predominance of primary sector, untapped energy resources, inefficient transport and communication systems, lack of entrepreneurship and marketing facilities etc. are the major factors for the slow growth of industrial activities. In order to develop this sector of economy the United Front government announced a separate industrial policy for the North-East India on December 24, 1997. But the present B.J.P.-led Government at the Centre has not only failed to offer additional incentives for starting of industries but has also neglected the task of execution of a separate industrial policy for the region formulated and announced by the predecessor government. Since the prospect of large and medium industries appears remote in the prevailing situation, the focus should be given to the promotion of small, cottage and tiny industries and other avenues like fostering of border trade and commerce with the neighbouring countries like Bangladesh, Myanmar, China and other South East Asian countries. Generally economic development of a region depends on people who live there and not on the abundance of natural resources. Now-a-days people of a particular region or a country are regarded as the basic resources for development and prime mover of economy. Thus training is an important component of human resource development strategy and such strategy should be oriented to the application of science and technology for improvement of job-oriented courses in some institutes in North-East India.

India including this region has so far completed eight Five Year Plans and is currently implementing the Ninth Plan, but hardly anything has been done to exploit the regional resources for the benefit of local people. In fact, development has neither affected the majority of indigenous people, nor modified their livelihood, in any significant way till today. There are 175 small urban centres, 8 cities and 44,531 villages in North East India. Generally the growth of cities and major urban centres is essentially a centre-down strategy of development in India and hence this strategy has no appeal for the bottom-up or development from below. But small urban centres constitute some important elements in the development process for both centre-down and bottom-up strategy which are now gaining currency everywhere. Thus the small urban centres of North-East India have a significant role in the face lift of the country especially to their surrounding rural areas. Economic viability and the future distribution of demand should be primary consideration for adopting a policy on planning for growth centres and regional development of North-East India. A development paradigm expresses relationship among economic variables which explains the events of past and predict future events under a set of simplifying assumptions. India's North-East lives in its villages and so planning strategy should aim at developing rural areas through the establishment of growth foci and through linking the different villages, service centres, and growth centres in an integrated manner. Special attention will have to be drawn on the building up of infrastructure, such as transport network, and means of communication and appropriate technology etc. The development strategy of the region lies on mutual understanding of different states. The economy of North-East India should be treated as a single economy with free inter-state flow of commodities. This development approach is essentially conceived as a special means to social ends. It has greater appeal to those who would like to achieve peaceful socio-economic changes.

REFERENCES

Bhooshan, B.S., 1980 (ed.), *Towards Alternative Settlement Strategies*, Heritage Publishers, New Delhi.

Datta Ray, B., 1990, 'Human Resource Development in North East', *The Assam Tribune*, (Friday, 12 November).

Wanmali, S., 1970, *Regional Planning for Social Facilities : A Case Study of Eastern Maharashtra*, Hyderabad, NICD.

11

PERSPECTIVE OF DEVELOPMENT

Sanjib Kumar Borkakoti

History has always been an unfailing teacher of the mankind. It has taught us that tyrannny does not last forever and that the beliefs cannot be suppressed by bullying tactics. The truth and inner goodness ultimately prevail. So the developmental strategists should take note of the fact that flower does not grow on corpses. The means is as important as the end. The disintegration of communist regimes all over the world and the compromises by the remaining ones prove the banality of the bloodshed witnessed by most of these regimes. It has now been proved that development does not come from the barrel of gun.

During the twenties and thirties, a massive agrarian reform had been undertaken in the then U.S.S.R. The fifteenth party Congress of the Communist Party held in 1927 approved the scheme of collectivization of agriculture in the country. The work was started in 1929. But it faced stiff resistance from the Kulaks. However the state did not succumb and retaliated by forcing the Kulaks to accept the collectivization programme. Not only that, the government went ahead to annihilate them. There was no incentive for the remaining farmers to work under the state as agricultural labourers in the collectivized farms. Consequently the agricultural productions fell. Millions of people died in the famine that followed in 1933. The hungry peasants killed half of their livestock for meat. Yet many died. Ultimately the Kolkhoz Congress of 1935 accepted the right of a family in the collective farm to private ownership of a plot of land.

By 1937, it was seen that the privately owned farms generated more cash income than the collective farms and state farms. But the private plots of land were only a quarter hectare to a half hectare in size.[1] Thus the small private farms proved to be more bountiful than the big state farms or collective farms. This proved the importance of private ownership and personal initiative in the production process. People do not deliver the goods when they are not free and somebody is breathing down their necks. The agricultural production data of USSR showed that the production in 1950 was lower than what had been a decade earlier.[2]

As usual in a developing economy, there was a rural to urban migration in USSR. Rural centres could no more offer any scope of employment, especially due to the policy of collectivization. Both the increasing unemployment and growing urbanization increased the urban population, which again became a cause of growing headache. With the policy of collectivization, the onus of feeding the urban populace came to lie on the state, which in turn increased the pressure on the agricultural sector. Perhaps the very move for collectivization was targeted at increasing the agricultural procurement so as to feed the process of industrialization and urbanization. But whatever was the cause and whatever the effect, they could work either way. Both reinforced one another and it became a vicious circle, from which the country could never come out. The USSR could never recover from these initial mistakes and the subsistence agriculture of the country remained forever in a low level equilibrium. The final disintegration of the USSR can be traced back to policy mistakes like this.

Contrary to this, China did not resort to an aggressive and violent programme in the agricultural sector. Yet the communist leadership stuck to their egalitarian principle and gave effect to the collectivization programme. But that was brought about in a smooth and peaceful manner. The violent activities took place during and in the sphere of cultural revolution, not while carrying out the collectivization programme. So, the collectivization programme, which took place between 1953 and 1956 did not disrupt the system and hence productions did not fall as in USSR. China did not go for excessive industrialization and urbanization. Because of her policy, there was no impelling reason for the rural people to migrate to the urban centres. She did not go for mechanization of her agriculture as USSR did. Yet her agricultural productions increased by 24.7 per cent during the period 1952 to 1957.[3] This augmentation of productions enabled the state to have a higher degree of primary accumulation. The state could appropriate the surplus from collectivized farms by agricultural taxes and through manipulation of terms of trade against agriculture.[4] Thus the Chinese government could make the agricultural sector help the industrial sector.

That peaceful programmes are more effective is also established by the fact that the rate of collectivization was much faster in China than in USSR. The actual work started in 1954 in China From 0.0001 per cent farm households collectivized that year, as many as 83 per cent were collectivized in 1956. Thus 83 per cent households were collectivized in just two years. But in USSR, the percentage of collectivized farm households increased from 0.8 per cent to 93 per cent in as many as ten years from 1927 to 1937. Even if we take a later year 1930 as the base year, 69.4 per cent households were collectivized in as many as seven years.[5] In any case, the speed of collectivization was more rapid in China than in USSR. The credits for that go to the better policy decisions and political programmes. That is why China is still going strong in a world where the bastions of communism have fallen one after another.

The comparative study of China and erstwhile USSR should be an eye-opener for the youths of the North-East India too. This backward and underdeveloped region has suffered in the hands of the rulers in New Delhi, who are impervious to the needs and aspirations of the people in this region.[6] So even after five decades of independence, this region has remained as poor as it was. In some economic parameters, the North-Eastern states have fallen into a worse position *vis-a-vis* rest of India. If all-India per capita income in 1980-81 is taken as the base level, the per capita income index of Assam fell from 103 in 1960-61 to 85 in 1970-71 and yet further to 70 in 1980-81, all in 1970-71 prices. From an excess of 40 points above the all-India per capita real income in 1950-51, the per capita real income of Assam gradually fell behind it and stood as much as 847 points below the all-India level in 1994-95, all measured in 1980-81 prices. Whereas 72.5 per cent people lived in villages in India in 1991, 88.1 per cent of the total population of Assam lived in villages.[7] Thus the economy of Assam is more rural and agriculture-based than the rest of India. The same is true about the other North-Eastern states too.

The continued underdeveloped condition of this region has induced many political outfits to clamour for rights of self-determination and even sovereignty. We can say it confindently that the revolutionary organizations of this region took to the path of struggle and insurgency because of this historic legacy. As their counterparts elsewhere, the insurgents of North-East also have been enamoured by communist ideology. In fact, the communist groups have encouraged and abetted extremism in North-East, like they do it everywhere.[8]

However, the extremists of Assam and North-East have failed to imbue the true spirit of communism. Several leaders had engaged themselves in high-sounding intellectual debates, but most of them ventured into exploitative economic ventures after renouncing the path of revolt. In fact the traders and producers have to fork out a large sum of money to appease the former revolutionaries, who have now turned into social parasites. The appropriation by these people have turned everything costlier thus raising the cost of living in Assam. All these prove that the youths are taking to armed struggle mostly out of frustration and due to insufficient opportunities of employment, rather than due to a deep commitment to their arowed cause. Naturally the armed struggle have not taken them anywhere, nor brought about any change in the socio-economic scenario of the state. The reason lies in the wrong selection of approach by these social deviants to tackle the problems of the state and its people. The same initiative, had it been carried out peacefully, would have worked reasonably just as it did in China.

Though we are not against any political philosophy, we may say that theoretically the socialist or communist polity would forever remain a utopia. The reason for this is the absence of any independent model to describe the functioning of socialist economy. The latter uses the same model as the capitalist economy and all its premises are based on the capitalist framework.[9] There are capitalists in both the systems. Whereas they are a fragmented lot in capitalism, the monolithic structure of the state itself functions as a capitalist in socialism. Whereas the individual owners of means of production appropriate the surplus of production in a capitalist economy, the state machinery appropriates it in a socialist economy. Therefore capitalism and socialism have no distinction in the ultimate analysis. And as a duplicate system, socialism is bound to fail. Little wonder, China has already made compromise with capitalism.

If our revolutionary youths realize this political fallacy, they would be restrained from turning to those political forces who have no other plan than to destabilize the socio-cultural system for their narrow political gain. We may do well to remember that even the Chinese politicians could not implement a perfect system; theirs was only a little better achievement than the Russian's. So twenty-nine million people perished in famine in China during the programme of 'Great leap forward', as was pointed out by the Nobel laureate Prof. Amartya Sen.[10] Thus China could not remain level-headed for ever and eventually committed the great Russian blunder. Our deviant youths should realize that these foreign countries cannot assist them to bring about an economic revolution in Assam. We need a proper and appropriate perspective of development, which cannot be imported from elsewhere but developed indigenously.

Any group or individual interested in the development of the North-East India should make it the primary task to study the nature of problems faced by this region. What are the infrastructural requirements of this region? Have the money earmarked for developmental works been spent properly ? Does the onus of underdevelopment lie squarely on the government alone? Are the entrepreneurs of this region equipped with the requisite dynamism or are they being thwarted by institutional bottlenecks? What are those commodities, which can be produced here locally? Is there a way to make the corrupt politicians and bureaucrats change their attitudes? We must ponder over these questions and explore rational solutions to the problems raised therein. Only then the developmental efforts would be equipped with proper direction, without which no revolution can succeed. It is because of lack of it that the members of extremist outfits become social parasites after returning to the mainstream of the society.

One of the most serious and burning problems of the North-East is the problem of unemployment. Lakhs of educated youths join the rank of unemployed every year. In 1986, a total of 2.86 lakh persons registered themselves as unemployed in 75 employment exchanges and university employment information and guidance bureaus of the North Eastern states. Out of these, as many as 2.09 lakh were registered in Assam.[11] The number of persons in the live registers of the employment exchanges in Assam increased to 13.56 lakh in 1991 and then to 14.29 lakh in 1992.[12] In view of insufficient development of secondary and tertiary sectors, the ever-increasing number of unemployed are increasing the pressure on the primary sector. All the North-Eastern states are predominantly agriculture-based economies. The availability of cultivable land per agricultural worker is going down due to increasing population and the consequent rise in rural work force. It was only 0.02 hectare in Assam in 1984-85 against all-India 1.12 hectares. Manipur was only slightly better at 0.36 hectare.[13]

Such a crisis situation has driven the youths of the region to the wall. And since a hungry man is as angry man, the North-East youths now see things in anger. However anger always burns the angry man himself the most. So the North-Easterners have suffered themselves in and due to innumerable agitations and struggles through the half century of independent era. The rest of the country have never bothered about the political upheavals in this region as long as the flow of raw materials from here remains undisturbed. The North-East is looked upon as the supplier of primary commodities for the secondary sector elsewhere, just the way India had been treated till half a century ago by the British. There is no use crying hoarse about his attitude. We have only wasted our precious time and energy which could have been utilized for manpower development, skill acquisition, primary capital formation and so on.

The need of the hour is to evolve a proper development perspective for this region and to inculcate it among the people. We, must have a clear vision of the ideal type of society unto which we want to transform ourselves. It is important to define the goal first if we have to attain it. Defining the goal and then pursuing it with dedication make the work half completed at the very outset itself.

What we should remember here is that our goal cannot be only material. A society comprises of both men and materials. And men do not live by bread alone. It is true that we need material developments like industrial growth to generate income and employment; we also need to increase foodgrain productions so that we can reduce the enormous imports from outside the state. But how all these are achieved is also equally important. The means is equally important as the end. Our work culture should reflect our wisdom, accumulated over the millenniums. We would do gross injustice to our own evolutionary process, if we behave like the denizens of forest to snatch our rightful dues. Nietzsche was wrong in saying that superman was not yet born.[14] Whenever a person attains fullness of life in both spirit and intellect, he/she can be said to have risen above the normal human level. We should also try to get over hatred and animosity against those who have wronged us, and derive our dues by developing our fullest potential.

Sri Aurobindo was very emphatic on this point. He believed that human beings could correct the limited knowledge of their minds by the use of "supramental truth-consciousness". This would help them grow out of their "still animal humanity into a diviner race".[15] He gave the humanity an integral *yoga* which aimed at evolution of men into higher levels. Self-perfection and work for the humanity enmeshed in ignorance and imperfections were his motto, just as was of Swami Vivekananda. Srimanta Sankardeva also exhorted people to give up demonic nature and to respect all creatures as embodiment of the supreme self.[16] These sermons have assumed a special significance in the present day Assam haunted by mutual hatred and inter-ethnic conflicts. Of course these universal truths hold good everywhere.

We should all therefore attempt to transcend our narrow sectarian interests and realize the perfect manhood in ourselves. An unbiased, unopinionated and liberal approach will enable us to solve any problematic issue that comes our way. The redeemer of all our woes is there within us. Those of us who can realize it will save both themselves and the society. The North-East should now see the birth of some selfless heroes. Let the present period be a transition from darkness to light, and a journey from ignorance to wisdom. Let the new millennium bring us true development.

NOTES

1. Modak, A. G., *Economic Development of the USSR,* 1982, pp. 78-81.
2. Dyker, D., *The Soviet Economy,* 1976, p. 125.
3. *ECKSTEIN*, A., *China's Economic Development,* 1989, p.24.
4. *Ibid.,* p. 249.
5. National Economy of the USSR, Statistical Handbook, p. 99. and *Tsu Kuo Weekly*, February 18, 1957, quoted in Eckstein, A., *op.cit.,* p. 251.
6. Dixit, J.N., No suitors for seven sisters, *The Telegraph,* October 26, 1998.
7. Borkakoti, S.K., *An Optimum Strategy for Industrialization in a Landlocked and Subsistence Agriculture Economy*, unpublished Ph.D, thesis, Gauhati University 1991: Statistical Handbook, Assam, 1996-97.
8. Borkakoti, S.K., Deshe bideshe bampanthir bhandami, and Bampanthir bisangati, in *Ajir Batori,* August 26 and September 16, 1998.
9. The author discussed the matter with late Prof. Krishna Bharadwaj, who was a leading political economist of the world. She concurred with the author on this issue. The author believes that the socialist countries use the same growth model as used by the capitalist countries.
10. However Prof. Sen did not compare China and Russia. He simply mentioned about the famine deaths in China. The comparison is of the present author.
11. Director General of Employment and Training, New Delhi, quoted in Basic Statistics, North Eastern Region, 1987, NEC Secretariat, Shillong, 1988.
12. Directorate of Employment and Craftsmen Training, Assam, Guwahati.
13. Data Bank 1989, *The Economic Times,* Calcutta 1989.
14. Nietzsche, F., Thus Spoke Zarathustra, quoted in Durant, W., *The Story of Philosophy,* 1977, p. 418.
15. Aurobindo, S., Sri Aurobindo on himself, Section V, quoted in Mitra, S., *Sri Aurobindo*, 1976, p. 181.
16. Sankardeva, Srimanta, *Kirtan Ghosha,* verse 359.

12

SHIFTING CULTIVATION IN NORTH-EAST INDIA : An Approach towards Control

D. N. Borthakur

Shifting cultivation, commonly known as *jhuming,* is one of the most ancient systems of farming believed to have originated in the Neolithic period around 7000 B.C. Shifting cultivation is also called the Slash and Burn method of cultivation. The system is regarded as the first step in transition from food gathering and hunting to food production. The method of cultivation has been called by different names locally in different countries or states. It is known as *Milapa* in Central America, *Coamile* in Mexico, *Conuco* in Venezuela, *Roka* in Brazil, *Masola* in Belgian Congo, *Chitemere* in some other parts of Central Africa, *Lavy* in Madagascar, *Taungya* in Burma, *Tamrai* in Thailand, *Ray* in Indo-China, *Karen* in Japan, *Ladang* in Indonesia, *Humah* in Java, *Diuma* in Sumatra and *Kaingin* in the Philippines. However in many of the above countries except the African ones, the area under this system is dwindling. It is of major concern in Orissa, Madhya Pradesh and states of the N.E. Region, although it is also practiced, though scantily, in Bihar, Andhra Pradesh, Kerala, Karnataka and Tamil Nadu. The method is known as Podu Cultivation in some parts of the country.

Shifting cultivation in the North Eastern Region is locally known as *jhuming*. It is widely prevalent in all the states of the region. According to the report of the National Commission on Agriculture (1976) 4,92,000 tribal families of this region are involved in *jhuming* and the total area affected by the practice is 26,94,000 ha., while 4,35,000 ha. remain under *jhuming* at any one time.

The System

The method followed in shifting cultivation is not exactly the same all over the world or even in the various states within India. However the essential features of shifting or slash and burn cultivation are the same in the sense that a virgin area is cleared by felling trees and buring these on site followed by mixed planting of seeds of various crops on the slopes without any soil conservation practice and finally shifting from one area to another after a few years. The essential features of *jhuming* as practiced in the North Eastern Region are :

(1) Selection of sites on hill slope usually before December. The mode of land allotment to individual families varies from tribe to tribe. It is mostly decided by village council (Mizo hills) or by village elders through lottery system (Manipur and Mikir hills) or by Nokma (Village chief) in Garo Hills etc. The plot size is decided on the basis of family size.
(2) Clearing of sites by cutting jungles in December-January.
(3) Burning of jungles around mid-February to mid-March.
(4) Planting of various crops in an intimate mixture by dibbling. Upland paddy is the main crop grown in mixture with maize, foxtail and finger millet, beans, cassava, yam, banana, sweet potato, ginger, cotton, tobacco, chillies, sesame, etc. A single crop of rice usually is preferred in second year of *jhuming*.
(5) Abandoning of land after 2 to 3 years of cultivation and shifting to another site for repeating the same process.
(6) The hutments of the village now remain at the same place in contrast to earlier days when the whole village shifted to the new site.
(7) Cropping is done with minimum tillage. No animal or large implement is used by the *jhum* cultivators for preparing land. The only implements used in farming are the chopping knife, the dibbling stick and a small hoe for weeding.
(8) There is practically no capital investment, except the labour and the seeds which usually come from the household.
(9) All operations, except cutting and burning of jungles, are usually performed by women.

The system of farming was the only alternative to sustain the people in the physical environment that prevailed in the hill slopes and when scientific technology was also not known. The system was also not harmful initially when it started and upto the time when the cycle of rotation was 10-15 years. The merits of the system were: (a) all crops required by the people could be raised in one operation, (b) the intimate mixture of crops provided a favourable crop canopy to check the erodible rains, (c) the soil was not much disturbed during planting as well as harvesting so as to reduce soil erosion, (d) the area available for shifting cultivation was abundant, due to scanty population and the virgin soil was fertile enough to ensure good yield, (e) rotation of 15-20 years (*jhum* cycle) provided adequate time gap for rehabilitation of soil. However, with growth of population and developments, the *jhum* cycle has now come down to 3-5 years and production from jhumland has gone down due to loss of fertility in soil. On the other hand, the life style of the people has changed greatly with growth of civilisation and other factors. Deforestation with related effects such as, soil erosion and removal of fertile top soil with useful microbes, disturbance in soil and water balance, floods in plains, loss of biodiversity etc. have led to ecological imbalance and degradation of the production base. These ecological disturbances will very adversely affect sustainable agriculture leading to problems in upgradation of the people. Thus, it is absolutely essential to repalce the system of farming so as to stop degradation of soil and water base, other related problems of environmental pollution, improve production, and standard of living of the people and their economy.

Attempts of Jhum Control

Attempts for controlling shifting cultivation were initiated around 1950-51 in the then undivided Assam. The various programmes taken up since then can be grouped under 3 broad categories as follows :

1. State Plans executed by soil conservation and forest department.
2. Centrally sponsored schemes and pilot projects.
3. Regional river basin schemes under N.E.C.'s programme. Programmes taken up under the above categories included schemes such as

    (i) Soil conservation schemes in the state sector.
    (ii) Plantation Crops Development Schemes.
    (iii) Centrally sponsored schemes of different types.
    (iv) Regional River basin Schemes under NEC.
    (v) Integrated *Jhumia* Development Project.
    (vi) Watershed Management Projects under N.E.C.
    (vii) Rehabilitation of *Jhumias.*
    (viii) Integrated Schemes for control of *jhuming* etc.

In spite of all these programmes, the desired success in *jhum* control has not been achieved. The rationale behind persistency of the system greatly lies in its compatibility with the physical environment —steep and undulating topography, land tenure system, socio-economic and cultural factors, lack of communication leading to physiographic remoteness and isolation etc.

It is not possible here to analyse the success or failure of every individual scheme in detail. However, a generalisation of the cause of failure of the scheme can be made. These include,

(i) Lack of awareness amongst the people.
(ii) Lack of adequate extension support.
(iii) Non-involvement of community and rural institutional infrastructure in decision making and execution.
(iv) Undue stress on development of terraces and poor production in dry terraces devoid of top soil due to lack of irrigation, growth of weeds and trying to raise rice in the upper terraces.
(v) In many cases, the entire village and the community were not covered under the programme leading to isolation of groups.
(vi) All crops raised by the farmers in *jhuming* were not included in the project laying stress on rice alone. Farmers resorted to *jhuming* for raising the other crops.
(vii) In case of watershed management projects, the schemes were drawn up theoretically without basing on the field/ground realities in terms of available labour/horse power, market etc.
(viii) Scientific land use and technology were not incorporated.
(ix) In case of plantation crops development the farmers were converted to wage earners without taking care of food security in the remote areas and hence farmers resorted to *jhuming* also.
(x) In case of Integrated *Jhumia* Development Project, lack of co-ordination among Government developments at the grassroot level was a major factor for failure of the project.
(xi) Lack of dedication and involvement of the executing personnel is, in general, an important factor for unsuccessful implementation of the schemes.

Research on Jhuming

The first ever attempt at systematic research on *jhuming* was initiated after establishment of the ICAR Research Complex for NEH Region. A multi-disciplinary research on shifting cultivation and farming systems based on watershed management were conducted with the objectives (a) to obtain all relevant data on various aspects of shifting cultivation, (b) to improve productivity and reduce/halt soil erosion without much upsetting the traditional *jhuming* and (c) to develop suitable watershed based farming systems to replace shifting cultivation.

Besides collecting data on tree felling, burning and soil erosion etc. the relevant findings of importance may be summarised as follows :

(i) Mixed land use is most ideal for hill slopes. Trees, horticulture, agriculture including fodder crops could be raised with scientific land use, livestock forming a subsidiary enterprise.

(ii) It is not necessary to terrace the entire hill slope as contourbund, vegetative bund and half-moon terraces can be effectively used depending on slope, crop etc.

(iii) It is possible to use 100 per cent local resources such as soil, bamboo, timber and manpower for developing suitable soil and water conservation measures as well as management of agriculture and livestock, so that farmers can locally and economically utilise technologies.

(iv) Water (run off) harvesting and preservation is feasible with earthen bunds for irrigation/life saving irrigation and fishery etc.

(v) While plannning crops in terraces, the concept of toposequence of crops should be utilised. Since moisture/water availability is more in the lower terraces, rice should be raised in lower terraces while crops such as maize, sesame etc. could be raised in the upper terraces.

(vi) In terraced land, the terrace risers, which constitute nearly 35-40 percent of land area, can be effectively utilised for raising perennial fodder grasses and legumes, which help in checking erosion besides providing feed for livestock.

(vii) Intercropping, multilayer cropping etc. are feasible to increase production.

(viii) Feasibility of various farming systems and their economics has also been worked out.

Two approaches were considered in the attempts to find solutions to the problem. These were (a) Improvement approach and (b) Replacement approach. The improvement approach could be used as the first step for changing to watershed based land use management, for improving production, and checking soil erosion in *jhuming*. This approach includes contour bunding, toposequential cropping use of improved varieties of crops and dibbling of fertilisers with seeds. The replacement method includes scientific treatment of land and use of farming systems based on watershed management incorporating viable technologies for agricultural production in hill slopes with the concept of mixed farming.

Socio-Economic Issues

It may be stated, at this stage, that programmes and technologies are now available to replace *jhuming* through other alternatives and watershed based farming systems is the most crucial strategy with promise. However, there are a number of socio-economic issues that need to be considered and attended to in order to achieve success. A survey was undertaken recently to study the socio-economic aspects of the farmers practising shifting cultivation. Thirty watersheds of six districts, taking 2 districts each from Assam, Meghalaya and Manipur. The findings of the survey taken up by R.R.A. methodology may be summarised as follows:

(i) Lower rate of adoption of settled agriculture is due to illiteracy, poverty and ignorance.

(ii) Efforts of the Development Departments is absolutely inadequate. In most cases, farmers in the interior areas have not seen any extension officer.

(iii) Farmers are aware of the declining production and the ill effects of *jhuming;* but they are not aware of alternative ways.

(iv) Wherever water is available, farmers invariably have taken up *"pani kheti"* (wet land rice). Similarly farmers are also raising some horticultural crops and livestock. These are very positive trend indicating that farmers are not averse to settled agriculture.

(v) Farmers also desire to have irrigation, but they cannot afford to develop the same.

(vi) Village headman/community chief are accepted as leaders.

(vii) Community bondage is very strong and the traditional institutions such as Village Development Committee headed by the headman (*Goanburah*) is very powerful. They are also willing to undertake responsibility. Such traditional institutional framework could be effectively utilised in execution of programmes.

(viii) Although women's participation in agricultural operations is rather high, yet there is still prejudice against women being members of the decision making committees such as V.D.C.

(ix) Village Development Committees had rigid rules for protection of trees/forests. For example, any individual can cut and use timber/ trees from the village forest only for construction of his house. V.D.C. can sell timber for raising funds for community expenses only. Otherwise, felling of trees is punishable by law. This healthy procedure should help in raising community forests. Fuel wood and minor forest products are, however, collected by farmers without felling trees.

(x) Dearth of schools, health care facilities, roads, transport and market are major handicaps for development. Some primary schools have, however, come up under the Christian Missionaries.

(xi) Production from *jhuming* is not adequate to meet the year round requirement of the families. Yet, some products, except rice, are marketed, sacrificing own consumption, to purchase other necessities such as salt, oil, clothes etc. Since there is no organised market nearby, road and transport facilities are also inadequate, the farmers do not receive reasonable price and are always at the mercy of the middle men.

(xii) Farmers are gradually changing their life style in their dresses and other ways, indicating that they want to change and raise their standard of living.

(xiii) Culture and traditions are linked with shifting cultivation. Rituals before shifting cultivation are practised by the entire community, even by those who have adequate area under settled agriculture, due to social ties and hence such persons also join in *jhuming*.

(xiv) Although existing land ownership is not conducive to permanent cultivation, yet there is an increasing trend of settling *"pani-kheti"* land against farmers who are practising the same.

Strategies for Controlling Jhuming

It would be evident from the above observations that just technology is not enough to wean away *jhumias* from this age old system of farming. A lot of considerations will be required in proper implementation of the programmes for achieving desired success. Similarly, there cannot be a single solution to the problem for all the states or for all the areas of even one state. Situations, hydrological behaviour of the areas, slope of the hill, needs of farmers and socio-economic condition of the farmers are all variable. The strategy for controlling shifting cultivation should, therefore, take into consideration the following measures and decide on the appropriate strategy suited to the situation and need of the farmers.

It should be remembered that it will not be possible to do away with *jhuming* in one stroke. Firstly, it is very deep rooted; and secondly, enormous efforts and money will be required. It will thus be worthwhile to phase the programmes based on priority. Endeavours to replace *jhuming* with alternate systems of farming should be taken up on a priority basis in areas where the *jhuming* cycle has come down to 3-5 years. In the areas where the cycle is 6 years and above and where replacement cannot be undertaken immediately, the improvement approach may be introduced immediately so as to gradually shift to alternate farming systems.

The alternative systems of farming, as recommended through research, are only bases for properly formulating projects suited to various agroclimates and situations after local survey :

(i) Massive awareness programmes need to be organised to make the farmers and farm women aware of the evil effects of *jhuming* and the scope for its replacement. Such programmes should also be specifically developed for village leaders, heads, clan chiefs, district councillors etc. who are the important agents in decision making.

(ii) Cultivation of plantation crops, such as rubber, depen ding on situation and provision of market. In such cases, the food security of the farmers have to be assured if they are engaged as wage earners for plantations, at least till the gestation period of the crop is over. Further, a clear understanding should be ensured that the crop will be handed over to the farmers within a specified period.

(iii) Large scale demonstration pilot projects on watershed management, even with micro watersheds should be taken up under both irrigated and unirrigated conditions. Research Scientists, Extension Officers and farmers need to be involved in such projects.

(iv) Farmers should be helped to carry out watershed based farming systems suited to the specific situations.

(v) Effective training programmes on watershed management projects. Women should be specifically trained as they carry out major activities in farming.

(vi) Regeneration of the degraded *jhum* land by raising plants like *alder* and perennial *arhar* etc.

(vii) Local resources such as soil, bamboo, timber etc. should be utilised for water harvesting, animal houses etc. so that farmers can use technology.

(viii) Public policies should be geared towards improvement and development of a conducive rural environment in respect of literacy, health care and infrastructures etc.

(ix) Success of programmes for weaning away farmers from *jhuming* will depend on :

(a) Involvement of farmers, rural institutional framework, V.D.C., village head/chief in decision making and execution of the programme.

(b) Such programme should cover entire community of the village/villages in the watershed.

(c) All crops raised by the farmers in *jhuming* should be included in the programme. Further livestock, horticulture, weaving, bee keeping and even fishery, where feasible, should form part of the programme.

(d) Irrigation, wherever feasible, should receive priority.

(e) Marketing should be organised in such a manner that the farmers receive reasonable price.

(f) Development Departments should act as catalysts only involving themselves in training, providing facilities of irrigation and market, supply of inputs and assisting farmers in decision making etc.

(g) All proven and appropriate technology must be incorporated in the programmes.

(h) Mechanism has to be developed to ensure effective co-ordination among the various departments involved in implementing the programmes.

(i) The executing personnel (extension officers) have to be thoroughly and appropriately oriented before taking up programmes in the rural areas.

The most important entry point to achieve success in involving farmers and executing the alternative farming systems are awareness, irrigation and market.

Research and Extension

As already mentioned, there cannot be a single solution for replacement of *jhuming*. Even a few stereotype farming systems will not provide all the answers, although these are the basic solutions in the right direction.

Research must be strengthened and geared up to find solutions to meet all the requirements of this multifaceted problems.

Survey convering all the states to identify specific problems in the interior areas should be carried out. This will help to formulate needbased research programme. Selection of crop for the farming systems will have to be based on the needs of the farmers, crops having assured market and crops fulfilling specific needs such as fodder etc. All crops raised by farmers in *jhuming* should be included in the research on farming system. Similarly, varieties of crops having different maturity period may have to be fitted into the system to suit specific situations. Farming system suited to irrigated as well rainfed conditions will have to be worked out. In addition to these, studies are needed in efficient management of soil and water use, and development of suitable tools and equipments for cultivation in terraces, proper use of biomass, recycling of wastes in various farming systems etc. Thus the scope of research on farming systems need to be enlarged to develop viable alternatives, which must be socially acceptable, so that farmers can choose a programme suited to their respective situations. Further, participatory research and extension have to be organized so that the technology can be modified to suit the requirements of farmers. Studies on marketing to suggest development of appropriate market strategy as well as on irrigation including indigenous systems for development of irrigation facilities in various situations deserve attention. Extension activities must be streamlined in order to wean away farmers from *jhuming*. Effective awareness programme, training and demonstration including participatory programmes need to be carried out to bring about community empowerment. Research scientists and extension workers will have to work as an unified team to ensure success.

Although the strategies outlined may not cover some other situations or specific problems, yet it is felt that once a beginning is made on the above lines success is bound to emerge.

REFERENCES

Abalu and Silva, D. Socio-economic Analysis of Existing Farming Systems and Practice in Northern Nigeria. *Proceedings of International Workshop on Socio-Economic Constraints to Development of Semi-Arid Tropical Agriculture,* Hyderabad, India 19-23 February, 1979.

Awasthi, R.P., Crop Production in Alternative Farming Systems : *Annual Report,* I.C.A.R. Complex, Shillong, pp. 13-17, 1977.

Awasthi, R. P.; Kari, S. and Grewal, J. S. : Effect of soil burning on the growth and yield of potato in Khasi Hills, Meghalaya, *Indian Jour. Agric.* Sci. 51 (5): 312-5, 1981.

Awashti, R.P.; Borthakur, D.N.: Agronomic Evaluation of rice varieties in upland terraces of Meghalaya : *Indian Journal of Agricultural Sciences* 56 (10):700-3 Oct, 1986.

Borthakur, D. N. : Improving Productivity of *jhum* cultivation with special reference to the North Eastern Hill Regions. *Indian Science Congress Association, 3rd Annual Session* Waltair, January 3-7, 1976.

Borthakur, D. N.; Awasthi, R.P. and Ghosh, S.P.: Alternative system of farming for increasing productivity in *jhum* lands. *Proceedings of Seminar on Shifting Cultivation in N. E. India.* North East India Council for Social Science Research, 1976.

Borthakur, D. N.; Singh, A.; Awasthi, R.P. and Rai, R.N.: Shifting Cultivation in North Eastern Region, *Proceedings of National Seminar on Resources Development and the Environment in the Himalayan Region.* Department of Science and Techonology, Government of India, 1978.

Borthakur, D.N.; Prasad, R.N. Ghosh, S.P.; Singh, A.; Awasthi, R.P.; Rai, R.N.; Verma, A.; Datta, H. H.; Sachan, J.N.; and Singh, M.D. : Agro-forestry based farming system as an alternative to *Jhuming* Seminar. *Proceedings on Agro-forestry organised by ICAR at Imphal,* Manipur, May, 1979.

Borthakur, D.N.; Singh, A.; Prasad, R.N.; *Shifting Cultivation in North East India and a Strategy for Land Water Resource Management:* Beitrage trop. Land wirtsch Veterinarmed: 23 H.2. 147-158, 1985.

ICAR Research Complex, Model Land Use—An Alternative to *Jhum* (Agricultural Extension Programme) *Extn. Folder No. 3,* 1980.

ICAR Research Complex, Shifting Cultivation in North East India: *Monograph No. 3*,1984.

Ingty, P.S.' and Goswami, N. : Shifting Cultivation in North Eastern Hills — A new approach to the problem. *Proceedings of the Agro-Forestry Seminar held at Imphal on May 16-18, Indian Council of Agricultural Research, 1979.*

International Crop Research Insitute for the Semi Arid Tropics: Farming system: Components for selected areas in India : Evidence from *ICRISAT : Research Bulletin No. 2 July, 1980.*

King, K.F.S. : Some Principles of Agro Forestry: Key Note address at the *ICAR Agro Forestry Seminar at Imphal, 1979.*

Mathur, S.: Shifting cultivation in the North Eastern Region. *Proceedings of the Agro-forestry Seminar held at Imphal on May 16-18, Organised by Indian Council of Agri. Res. 1979.*

Mawthoh, P.R. : Shifting Cultivation in Meghalaya: paper presented at the *Seminar on Shifting Cultivation in the North Eastern States by N.E.C., May, 1989.*

Singh, A: Shifting cultivation and Soil Erosion Problems in North Eastern Hill Region. Paper presented in *XVI Annual Convention of ISAE held at IIT, Kharagpur, 1978.*

Singh, A., and Singh, M.D. : Effect of various stages of shifting cultivation on soil erosion from steep hill slopes. *Indian Forester : 106 (2) 115-121, 1978.*

Varma, Arun; Yadav, B.P.S.; Sampath, K.T. and Borthakur, D. N. : Feeds and Feeding habits in North Eastern Hills, Part-II: Cultivated Fodder Production, Conservation and Utilization : *Res. Bulletin No. 18, ICAR Res. Complex, 1982.*

13

HUMAN DEVELOPMENT IN NORTH-EAST INDIA

R.P. Bhattacharjee and *N. Upadhaya*

Introduction

In the 21st century, the crucial challenge of North-Eastern states will be how to strike a balance of the economy of the region with that of rest of India *vis-a-vis* the world and also to ensure ecological balance. After the re-organisation of North-East, the economy has developed rapidly, the living standard of the people has been enhanced. But it was not enough to match the national standard. During pre-independence era, the natural resources have been overexploited for the development of rest of India — be it fossil fuel or evergreen forest products. The plight and plethora had not changed during second half of this century as British legacy continued to exploit and deprive this beautiful land — a nature's bounty.

The North-East has 7.8 per cent of geographical area of the country with a population of 3.7 per cent but only 2.8 per cent of foodgrain is produced in the region. While the share of NDP is only 2.5 per cent though the workers' share is much higher (3.7%). This shows that the productivity and efficiency of workers in the region is not encouraging compared to rest of India, whereas human-resource of the region is not at all inferior to others as literacy in the region is 54.5 per cent compared to 52.2 per cent of national rate. This region is full of natural resources be it water resource, mineral resource or natural resource. For example, the region accounts for 25.9 per cent of forest area of the country. Over the years deforestation and overgrazing have caused tremendous land erosion and landslides, but this is perhaps more in rest of India compared to this region. It may be pointed out that the region has 64.3 per cent of forest cover compared to 19.33 per cent in all India. The forest provides us many things of our daily use such as food, timber, firewood, pulp, forage, fibre, medicinal plants, etc., and also plays a critical role in maintaining ecology of the region. Already 1734 sq. km. of forest area has been lost in the region during 1990s. For the sake of development, we cannot denegrade the ecology of the region. This environmental crisis creating the genetic erosion of flora, fauna and the depletion of natural resources, perhaps, can be minimised by minimising the Demand-Supply gap of forest product and this can be done by restricting population growth and proper human resource development.

The Concept

The real wealth of the nation is its people. The basic purpose of development is to create environment for the people to enjoy long, healthy and creative lives. But we often forget this powerful truth in the persuit of material and financial gain. The result is destruction and diminishing of our natural resources, which must be combated.

The liberalization process in our economy has helped to reach a higher growth rate in 1990s and it is through the development of agriculture and industry where maximum of our manpower are engaged. But this has not developed equitably in our country. The blessings of green revolution has helped Punjab and Haryana to establish as foodgrain bowl of India. This has helped them to become one of the most developed states of India, attain growth and per capita income. But this is not so in the case of North-East Region; as a result human development has suffered. The UNDP has introduced a broad approach to improve human well-being covering all aspects of human-life for both rich and poor countries.

The UNDP introduced the Human Development Index (HDI) in 1990 and since then it is observed that the GDP and HDI is having a positive correlation in India. Perhaps it is true for North-East India too but due to lack of any report or estimate of HDI for North-Eastern Region is difficult to make critical assessment. With the present paradigm, Human Development is the only alternative to have sustainable development.

Sustainable Development

Sustainable development is a familiar term to many people and governments throughout the world ever since it was for the first time discussed at World Environment Congress 1987. There are divergent views on the meaning of sustainable development but widely acceptable concept is "Human development" without damaging environment and without disturbing the rights of future generations. Hence this needs an analysis of Human Development parameters.

Human Development

"Human development", according to Prof. Paul Streeten, "is the process of enlarging people's choices not just choices among different detergents, television channels or car models but the choices that are created by expanding human capabilities and functionings — what people do and can do in their lives. At all levels of development a few capabilities are essential for human development, without which many choices in life would not be available. These capabilities are to lead long and healthy lives, to be knowledgeable and to have access to the resources needed for a decent standard of living and these are reflected in the human development index. But many additional choices are valued by people. These include political, social, economic and cultural freedom, a sense of community, opportunities for being creative and productive, and self-respect and human rights. Yet human development is more than just achieving these capabilities, it is also the process of pursuing them in a way that is equitable, participatory, productive and sustainable". Human development includes the expansion of income and wealth, but it includes many other valuable things as well. These are adequate nutrition, safe water, better health care, better schooling, cheap transport, adequate shelter, employment to secure livelihoods. Mere productivity, remuneration, satisfying jobs for few do not show higher income for all, even though economic health of the country may be good.

There are other non-material benefits that are often more highly valued by poor people than material improvements. Some of these partake in the characteristics of rights, others in those of states of mind. Among these are good and safe working. Conditions, freedom to choose jobs and livelihoods, freedom of movement and speech, liberation from oppression, violence and exploitation, security from persecution and arbitrary arrest. A satisfying family life, the assertion of cultural and religious values, adequate leisure time and satisfying forms of its use, a sense of purpose in life and work, the opportunity to join and actively participate in the activities of civil society and a sense of belonging to a community. These are often more highly valued than income, both in their own right and as a means to satisfying and productive work. They do not contribute to higher income but certainly help to form a congenial society. No policy makers can guarantee the achievement of all, or even the majority of these aspirations, but policies can create the opportunities for their fulfilment. Let us therefore nurture the new ethos of UNDP — the Human Development Indices.

Human Development Indices

Since first published in 1990, Human Development Reports have developed and constructed several composite indices to measure different aspects of human development. The human development index (HDI) has been constructed every year since 1990 to measure average achievements in basic human development in one simple composite index and to produce a ranking of countries. The gender related development index (GDI) and the gender empowerment measure (GEM), introduced in Human Development Report, 1995 are composite measures reflecting gender inequalities in Human Development while the GDI captures achievement in basic human development adjusted for gender inequality, the GEM measures gender inequality in economic and political opportunities. Human Development Report 1997 introduced the concept of human poverty and formulated a composite measures of it — the human poverty index (HPI). While the HDI measures average achievement in basic dimensions of human development, the HPI measures deprivations in those dimensions. These are shown in Table 13.1.

Human Development Index in North-East

Differences in human development exist not only between countries and between North and South. Any country's human development data, disaggregated by region, gender, ethnic group or rural and urban areas, reveal significant disparities within countries. And disparities of all kinds are interrelated and overlapping. And these disparities are observed in North-East also. R.P. Bhattacharjee estimated HDI of a few states including Arunachal Pradesh and Assam with 1991-92 data base. Arunachal Pradesh was having HDI value of 0.28 and Assam had 0.21. The HDI of other states were as follows: Kerala (0.75), Punjab (0.70), Maharashtra (0.61), Haryana (0.58), Himachal Pradesh (0.48), Gujarat (0.45), Karnataka (0.45), Tamil Nadu (0.42), West Bengal (0.37), Andhra Pradesh (0.32), Orissa (0.18), Madhya Pradesh (14.5), Rajasthan (14.5), Uttar Pradesh (0.07) and Bihar (0.05). Thus we find significant disparities in India.

North-East is perhaps, the most poor region in respect of availability of data and information about different aspects of socio-economic parameters. For example, we do not have life expectancy data for all the N.E. states. Due to this, we have substituted life expectancy for all ages by infant survival rate to estimate HDI of all the seven states along with the remaining parameters of literacy above 7 years of age and per capita real Net State Domestic Product.

It is felt that adult literacy rate and mean years of schooling combined at the ratio two-thirds and one-third respectively can better represent the

Table-13.1 : HDI, GDI, HPI — Dimension and Measurements

Index	Longevity	Knowledge	Decent Standard of living	Participation or exclusion
HDI	Life expectancy at birth	1. Adult literacy rate 2. Combined enrolment ratio	Adjusted per capita income in PPP $	—
GDI	Female and male life expectancy at birth	1. Female and Male adult literacy rate 2. Female and male combined enrolment ratio	Adjusted per capita income in PPP $ based on female and male earned income shares	
HPI-1 For developing countries	Percentage of people not expected to survive upto age 40	Adult illiteracy rate	1. Percentage of people without access to safe water. 2. Percentage of people without access to health service. 3. Percentage of under-weight children under five.	
HPI-2 For Indus-trialized countries	Percentage of people not expected to survive upto age 60	Adult functional illiteracy rate	Percentage of people living below the income poverty line (50% of median personal disposal income)	Long term un-employment rate (12 months or more.)

Source : UNDP, HDR, 1999, p. 127.

level of education as proposed by the UNDP in the modified version of the index. But necessary data for estimating mean years of schooling for 1991 are not available. For this reason, literacy rate above seven years is taken here for estimating HDI.

For the health component, infant survivial rate is chosen which is defined by infant survival per thousand live births. This is chosen because data on life expectancy are not available for all the N.E. states except Assam.

In the modified HDI by the UNDP, diminishing marginal utility of income is made progressive above the poverty line income by the use of the notion of elasticity of marginal utility of income with respect to income. This could not be done in this study due to lack of state level data in this regard. Hence, this chapter assumes unitary elasticity of marginal utility of income with reference to income.

While estimating the HDI, the maximum and minimum values of all states in India is taken into account. The deprivation index of the three components are averaged with equal weights to obtain the average deprivation indicator. And lastly, the average deprivation indicator is subtracted from one to get HDI. These are shown below:

Table 13.2 Deprivation Index and HDI in North-East India

States	Deprivation Index		Real per capita NSDP (1996)		HDI
	Literacy (1991)	Infant survival rate (1991)	Deprivation Index	Average Deprivation Index	
1	2	3	4	5	6
Arunachal Pradesh	0.94	0.66	0.28	0.63	0.37 (4)
Assam	0.72	0.69	0.86	0.76	0.24 (7)
Manipur	0.58	0.03	0.78	0.46	0.54 (2)
Meghalaya	0.80	0.57	0.84	0.74	0.26 (6)
Mizoram	0.15	0.32	0.39	0.29	0.71 (1)
Nagaland	0.55	0.28	0.71	0.51	0.49 (3)
Tripura	0.57	0.59	0.77	0.64	0.36 (5)
All India	0.71	0.54	0.58	0.61	0.39

Note : Rank of HDI shown in parentheses.

We find that Mizoram ranks 1st and Manipur ranks 2nd in HDI in North East while Nagaland is 3rd, Arunachal Pradesh is 4th, Tripura is 5th, Meghalaya is 6th and Assam is 7th rank in HDI. We find lot of variation in literacy from 0.15 (Mizoram) to 0.94 (Arunachal Pradesh), and in infant survival rate from 0.03 (Manipur) to 0.69 (Assam) and per capita NSDP from 0.28 (Arunachal Pradesh) to 0.86 (Assam).

Thus estimation of HDI in this chapter reveals that the extent of relative deprivation in Assam is more compared to other states. It is relatively high in Meghalaya also. Compared to all-India, the states of Tripura and Arunachal Pradesh have slight lower HDI while Mizoram, Manipur and Nagaland are relatively in better position.

Suggestions

It has been stated earlier that there is shortage of essential data for estimation of HDI or other indices or even to prepare HDRs. The Planning Commission has already appealed to the State Governments to prepare Human Development Reports (HDRs) for their respective states to make the planning process more effective.

It is suggested that the States Directorates specially the Directorate of Economics and Statistics may be insisted to provide and publish latest data on all socio-economic parameters. The information of income, literacy (both male and female), enrolments (%), life expectancy at birth and all single age, percentage of people having access of drinking water, sanitation, health services, population under BPL both at rural and urban, male and female, weights of children at all ages etc. may be collected sincerely. This will help social scientists to prepare all Human Development Indices. The Government can have proper planning process for eradication of illiteracy, hunger, unemployment, deprivation, inequality etc. The State Governments in this region should prepare HDRs annually and publish it in a fixed and time bound period. If possible, District level HDRs may also be prepared.

The objective of maximum utilisation of human capital in the year to come could be by maximising the growth of GSDP, total literacy and best health care facility in all villages of North-East. It is also suggested that the data could be collected also through Project Study given to Academic Institutions and also to NGOs.

REFERENCES

Basabi Bhattacharya, "Urbanisation and Human Development in West Bengal" in *EPW,* Vol. XXXIII Nos. 47 and 48, Nov. 21 - Dec. 4, 1998, pp. 3027-3032.

Bhattacharjee, R.P., "Economic Development of Arunachal Pradesh" Unpublished Ph.D. Thesis, G.U. 1997, p. 277 and "Human Development Index in Arunachal Pradesh", *The Arunachal Times,* 8 August, 1999.

Census of India, 1991.

EPW – Research Foundation, "National Accounts Statistics of India 1950-51 to 1995-96" (p. 76).

Forest Survey of India, "State of Forest Report, 1997".

HDR, 1999 UNDP, (p. 127).

Ibid., (p. 17).

IIPS, National Family Health Survey 1992-93, Bombay (Fact sheet state findings).

NEC (1995), *Basic Statistics of North Eastern Region,* p. 59 (Shillong).

Paul Streeten in Human Development Report 1999, UNDP, Oxford University Press, (p.16).

Rajan, S.I. and P. Mohanachandran, "Infant and Child Mortality, Estimates" -Part I, *EPW* — Vol. XXXIII No. 19, May 9-15, 1998, pp. 1120-1140.

The Arunachal Times, 2nd August, 1999.

14

POPULATION GROWTH AND ENVIRONMENTAL CRISIS IN NORTH- EAST INDIA : Problems and Remedies

P. C. Dutta

Introduction

For the past over 200 years, scholars and policy makers have been debating the question of the relationship between population and development. Perhaps the best known controversy is that between the doomsayers who see the concurrent pressures of population growth, increased demand for resources and environmental degradation as serious threats to the earth's capacity to sustain human population. On 11th July 1987, the world population touched the five billion mark and will be over 6 billion by the year 2000 with almost ninety per cent of growth taking place in the developing countries. The third world, which constitutes nearly 70 per cent of the total world's population, subsists on only 20 per cent of the world's income. Even this meagre income is so maldistributed internally that a bulk of their population is in abject poverty. Economic and social forces, both internal and external, are responsible for poverty, inequality and low productivity that commonly characterize most third world countries.

Realizing the negative effect of rapid population growth on development, many developing countries have launched family planning programmes. But in a majority of countries, including India, family planning programmes have not been so successful. Population is a very important factor in the whole process of socio-economic development. While the growing population in developing and under developing countries, in particular, is straining social, economic and even political system of the nation. At the 5th World population conference, held in Mexico city (5th September, 1994), 76 decisions were made to improve the standards of living and quality of life for all people among which socio-economic development, the environment, the population and the environment, the role and status of women etc. were given the priority (APRET, 1998).

In her inaugural address at the first conference of Asian Forum of Parliamentarians for Population and Development held at New Delhi, 17-20 February, 1984, Mrs. Indira Gandhi, the then Prime Minister of India made a special reference to importance of education in inculcating attitudinal and behavioural changes in the people to accept family planning. Young people must be in the vanguard of the movement to restrict population growth and to promote sustained development. The development of an area is best reflected in the quality of life of its people. Quality of life is a very complex concept and perceived and interpreted differently by different people depending upon their socio-cultural and religious background, personal preferences and their philosophy of life. The quality of life is the sense of being pleased or satisfied with those life elements that are most important to a person. In addition, quality is the sense of being pleased with what one has. The quality of life involves the satisfaction of the emotional needs and social aspirations of the community or society as well as the society's ability to meet the basic needs of food, energy, space, housing etc. by itself. Apart from the distribution of infrastructural facilities, the quality of life depends upon several other factors like geographical, ecological, socio-cultural etc., which are distributed in a haphazard manner all over the country and thus handicaps the development of relatively backward regions. Historical and political conditions also affect the socio-economic development of the region.

Urbanisation, a phenomenon closely related with burgeoning population, has swallowed up approximately 1.5 million hectares of agricultural land in the past 30 years. In addition 1.3 million hectares of forest was lost each year during 1975-82. The shortage of housing is an ever-growing problem. Over one-fifth of the urban population lives in slums. The mounting problems of pollution consequent upon unimaginative interference of human beings with nature have been adversely affecting the quality of life. Forests provide several products of daily use such as food, timber, fire wood, wood pulp etc. apart from different medicinal plants which are yet to be explored. The greatest significance of forests, however, lies in their critical role in maintaining ecological processes and life supporting systems (Singh and Sudarshan, 1996). Various studies on Indian urbanisation reveals that, Indian cities are expanding on the one hand and losing green field areas on the other, with disastrous ecological crisis in our towns and cities. The deterioration of the environmental quality is regarded as the inevitable consequence of urbanisation.

Urbanisation is a process of population concentration. We have conceded the Kingsley Davisian view in the 19th century that "it is not possible to have industrialisation without urbanisation". It is fact that the urbanisation is the most essential for all-round development of the developing nations, as it has increased employment, income and standard of living in these countries. But it has simultaneously created number of socio-economic and environmental problems. Urbanisation has disturbed the ecological balance by creating air, water and noise pollution through industrialisation. Haphazard growth of urban centres and their ill-planned urbanisation aggravated the pollution problems and deteriorated the environment. Therefore, environmentalists aptly say that urbanisation-environment relationship is not complementary but contradictory with each other (Patil, 1998).

The increasing urbanisation has led to a number of socio-economic problems like crime, suicides, drug abuse, unemployment and poverty, alcoholism, overcrowding, housing shortage, slums, traffic control and pollution etc. At the same time they are also centres of civilisation and culture by helping a lot in the process of modernisation (Dutta & Pradhan, 1998). The very pattern of economic development in the third world countries has resulted increasing imbalance in the distribution of per capita national income and large number of people are being relegated to below poverty line. The poor occupy the environmentally vulnerable areas liable to water logging or flooding, other natural hazard, epidemics, fire and chemical pollution. Economic development not only brings about changes in the socio-economic and cultural life of a population but it also influences the consumption pattern in the long run (Dutta, 1996).

Poverty is the worst form of environmental degradation because it forces an extremely substandard quality of life upon a large segment of society and causes deprivation from such basic needs of human existence as shelter, nutrition, hygiene and health service, education, safe drinking water, sanitation and other physical infrastructure.

Growing global environmental concern on one hand and policy of infrastructural changes aimed at promoting growth on the other bring the traditional debate on the trade off between growth and environmental to the force. Past experience has shown that while India has vigorously persuaded a policy of industrialisation and urbanisation following the western models, scant attention was given to industrial and municipal wastes and control of hazardous wastes and substances (Dutta & Roy, 1998).

Education plays a very important role in promoting economic, social, political and institutional development. Education promotes development of all the sectors including agriculture, industry and social sector. Rather the social returns to education far more outweigh the economic returns and the social rate of return is highest in case of primary education followed by secondary and higher education (Pracharopouclus, 1994).

There is a worldwide concern over the damage to environment. The greedy men have been drifting away more and more from the nature and the degree of departure from nature becomes the yardstick to measure the so called development and civilization which have been made possible only to the great detriment of nature. There has been massive intervention in the environment without quite understanding its complications. The demand for more and more resources has been ever-increasing. Such a process of resource exploitation has now brought about a situation where nature is in danger which is called environmental or ecological crisis.

Aims and Objectives

It is in this context, that an enquiry is deemed to be necessary into the population-environment fabric of the North-East India. In this chapter an attempt has been made to examine the complex and multi-dimensional relationships among some socio-economic variables. The purpose of the study is to examine whether or how urbanisation creates the hazardous situation in socio-economic aspects. Further, the study shows how population growth affects overall environment of the region. Lastly, a few remedial measures to the created problems have been put forward in order to maintain the ecological balance in North-East India.

Data

The work is based on secondary data relating to socio-economic and demographic variables for the North-Eastern Region of India, published by the Ministry of Welfare, Government of India (1985, 1995), Population Foundation of India (1998), Statistical Abstract (1998), Central Water Commission (1992), Rural Health Statistics, Ministry of Health and Family Welfare, Government of India (1995), and different rounds of NSS data on consumer expenditure.

Profile

The topography of NER is not uniform. Mountains, rivers and barren hilly terrain remain as problems rather than prospect for development. Geographically, the region is lying between 21° 5' north latitude and 85°5'

- 97°5' east longitude covering an area of 2,55,037 sq. km (7.7% of nations's land), 70 per cent of which is hilly with more than 80 per cent population living in the rural areas.

The strategic importance of this region is highly significant as it borders neighbouring countries like Bangladesh, Myanmar, Tibet, Nepal and Bhutan. However, the region is endowed with rich resources of land, water, forests, minerals. Anyone would have thought that such a typical region would have been cherished pride of the country, instead it is the most backward and underdeveloped one. One must realise that North-East India is a mini India. There are more than 74 major population groups and subgroups, speaking approximately more than 400 languages and dialects, of which there are about 168 in Arunachal Pradesh, 95 in Nagaland, 87 in Manipur, 100 in Tripura and 200 in Assam, Meghalaya and Mizoram (Madhab, 1999).

Analysis

The total population of the region is about 31.54 million, representing 3.73 per cent of India's total population. From Table 14.1, it is evident that there is uneven spatial distribution of population among the constituent states. For example, Assam, second in terms of area contains 71.05 per cent of the region's population whereas Mizoram less than 3 per cent (2.18 per cent) of the regional population stands at the other extreme. The region's growth rate of population is much higher than the national average. India is the second most populated country in the world. The population of India has been estimated at 971.8 million as on 1st July, 1998 showing an increase of more than 124.5 million since the last census conducted in 1991 which was 846.3 million.

Table 14.1 : Population Trend in North-East Region (in '000)

State	1951	1961	1971	1981	1991	1998*
Arunachal Pradesh	—	337	468	632	865	1128
Assam	8029	10837	14625	18041	22414	25646
Manipur	578	780	1073	1421	1837	2385
Meghalaya	606	769	1012	1336	1775	2305
Mizoram	196	266	332	494	690	901
Nagaland	213	369	516	775	1210	1591
Tripura	639	1142	1556	2053	2757	3582
N E R	10260	14501	19582	24752	31547	37539
India	361088	439235	548160	683329	846303	971832

* Estimates based on mid-year population (as on 1st July).

It is interesting to note that India's total population increased by about 54.39 per cent between 1971-1991 whereas for North-East, the growth was 62 per cent. The region's population growth was not only high in pre-independence period but maintained the trend thereafter. Comparing 1991 with 1951, India's population increased by 134 per cent while for the region it was 208 per cent. No doubt, the existing population of each state is a matter of concern, but the more important is the fast growing population in some of the states of the region. At the same time, there is a large variation in the density of population among the North-Eastern states (Table 14.2). Density of region's population is almost half (147.88 per cent) of the national density of 307 in 1998 while it was only 35.09 per cent in 1951. The bulk of population of the region is concentrated mainly of three sectors, viz. Brahmaputra valley and Barak valley of Assam, Tripura and Imphal. The large variation is caused by the geographical and economic factors which vary greatly within the region. Another important factor is the migration causing higher densities in Assam and Tripura in particular.

Table 14.2 : Population Pattern in the States of NER and India

State	Population per Sq.Km.			ST Population (in p.c.)		Sex - Ratio		Rates of urbanisation (in p.c.)	
	1951	1991	1998	1981	1991	1981	1991	1981	1991
Arunachal Pradesh	—	10	14	69.82	63.7	862	859	6.56	12.80
Assam	102	184	327	—	12.82	910	923	9.89	11.10
Manipur	26	82	107	27.3	34.4	971	958	26.42	27.52
Meghalaya	27	79	103	80.6	85.5	954	955	18.07	18.60
Mizoram	9	33	43	93.6	94.8	919	921	24.67	46.10
Nagaland	13	73	96	84.0	87.7	863	886	15.52	17.21
Tripura	61	263	342	28.4	30.9	946	945	10.99	15.30
N E R	40	124	147	—	25.71	921	925	11.76	13.89
India	117	273	307	7.53	8.01	934	927	23.31	25.71

*Estimates based on mid-year population (as on 1st July).

The urban population in India has been estimated at 268.8 million as on 1st March 1998. The 1991 census figure was 217.2 million. It has been projected to increase to 425 million in 2016 or an increase of 208 million during a period of 25 years, i.e. the urban population would almost double in 25 years (Table 14.2).

Coming to the states of NER, the notable point is that the percentage of urban population to total population (urbanization) varies from 12.80

(Arunachal Pradesh) to 46.10 (Mizoram). It is striking to note that except Manipur (27.52 per cent) and Mizoram, all other states of NER are below the national percentage of urbanisation (25.71 per cent) according to 1991 census. The urbanization in India is structurally imbalance and is going to maintain the same trend unless there is a policy intervention to reorient the urbanisation trend in favour of small and medium size towns along with metropolitan decentralization (Pathak, 1998). The percentage of population in the region with respect to India was 1.79 per cent in 1901, 2.70 in 1941, 2.84 in 1951 and 3.86 in 1998, showing an increasing trend of population growth in the region with respect to India.

The percentage of tribal population in NER (Table 14.2) is 25.71 per cent of total population. The percentage of scheduled tribes varies from 13 per cent (Assam) to 97 per cent (Mizoram) which are above the national percentage of tribal population (8 %). More than three-fourths of the households belong to scheduled tribes in the states of Mizoram, Nagaland (96%), Meghalaya (89%) and Arunachal Pradesh (76%).

Sex-ratio is an important determinant of population growth. Among the states of NER, it is highest in Manipur (958) followed by Meghalaya (955) and Tripura (945) while other states are lying below the national level of 927 females per 1000 males in the total population (Table 14.2).

The age distribution in each state of NER is typical of high fertility population with a high proportion of the population in the younger age groups. Manipur, Mizoram and Tripura have the lowest percentage of population below 15 years of age (39 %) and this percentage is the highest in Arunachal Pradesh (43 %). The proportion of the population of age 65 and above varies from just over 2 per cent in Nagaland to 6 per cent in Tripura (Table 14.3).

Table 14.3 : Distribution of Population according to Age Groups (dependency), Female Work Participation and Infant Mortality Rate in the N.E. States and India

State	Population 0-4 Years old (in p.c.)		Population 65+ years old (in p.c.)		Female work participation (in p.c.)		Infant mortality rate
	1981	1991	1981	1991	1981	1991	1991
Arunachal Pradesh	39.4	43.3	2.6	2.7	40.55	37.5	64
Assam	39.8	39.6	4.2	4.4	—	21.6	83
Manipur	39.3	36.6	3.6	4.0	34.59	39.0	24
Meghalaya	42.4	42.2	2.5	2.1	32.29	34.9	58
Mizoram	39.6	36.6	2.9	3.2	32.33	43.5	—
Nagaland	36.8	41.3	3.9	1.3	42.45	38.0	10
Tripura	39.4	37.1	4.5	5.5	8.95	13.8	51
India	39.6	39.8	3.8	4.2	13.99	22.3	79

Female work participation rate is much higher in the states of NER except in Tripura (9 %) which is below the national level (14 %). In the other states of NER, the percentage varies from (32 %) in Meghalaya to 43 per cent in Nagaland (Table 14.3).

Education is the main instrument of social change. There are some notable features of this region. Except Arunachal Pradesh (42 %) and Meghalaya (49 %), the literacy level of the region's population is above the national level (52 %) according to 1991 census (Table 14.4). While according to 1997, except Arunachal Pradesh (60 %), all the states of NER, ranges from 73 per cent to 95 per cent, are above the national literacy rate (62 per cent).

The female literacy rate is the highest in Mizoram (95 %) followed by Nagaland (77 %) and lowest in Arunachal Pradesh (48 %) followed by Assam and Manipur (66 % in each case.) Arunachal Pradesh is the only state in NER in which female literacy rate is below the national figure of 50 per cent. There is a big gender gap in literacy which is one of the major obstacles in attaining total literacy (Table-14.4). The highest gender gap is observed in the states of Manipur (24.03 %), Arunachal Pradesh (21.76%), Tripura (20.93%) and lowest in Mizoram (7.01%) followed by Meghalaya (8.27 %). However, all the states of NER are below the all-India level of 24.84 per cent points. Low female literacy has strong repercussions on other aspects like enrolment of children, population growth, child care and acceptance of family welfare measures.

Table 14.4 : Female Literacy Rate, Total Literacy, Gender Gap in Literacy and Per Capita Expenditure on Education by the Government of different N.E. States

State	Female literacy rate (in p.c.)		Total literacy (in p.c.)		PCE (Govt.) on education (in Rs.)		Gender gap in literacy
	1981	1991	1991	1997	1991-92	1997-98	1991
Arunachal Pradesh	30	48	42	60	549	951	21.76
Assam	43	66	53	75	250	537	18.84
Manipur	48	66	60	76	560	984	24.03
Meghalaya	45	74	49	77	406	779	8.27
Mizoram	79	95	82	95	769	1210	7.01
Nagaland	55	77	62	84	437	762	12.87
Tripura	50	67	60	73	416	836	20.93
India	39	50	52	62	—	—	24.84

It is striking to note that per capita expenditure of education in 1997-98 is the highest for smaller states of Mizoram (Rs. 1210), Manipur (Rs. 984), Arunachal Pradesh (Rs. 951) and Tripura (Rs. 836) while it is only Rs. 537 in Assam which is the lowest among the states of NER (Table 14.4). To have a rough idea about the economic condition of the people of NER with respect to India, per capita net state domestic product of different states have been shown in Table 14.5. A close look at the table, it reveals that all the states except Arunachal Pradesh (Rs. 2119 - Rs. 3265) and Mizoram (Rs. 2119 - Rs. 7743) of NER are below the all-India level (Rs. 1857 - Rs. 2553) for the years 1985-86 to 1994-95. It is to be noted that in 1980-81, PCNDP for all the states of NER, were below the all-India level (Rs. 1625). In this respect Assam's position is the lowest for ever during the period 1990-91 (Rs. 1544) to 1996-97 (Rs. 1628) and also in the period 1980-81 (Rs. 1284), among the states of NER. The picture shows the economically backwardness of NER and Assam, in particular, with respect to all-India level.

Table 14.5 : Per Capita Net State Domestic Product (At Current Prices 1980-81) (in Rs.)

State	1980-81	1985-86	1990-91	1994-95	1995-96	1996-97
Arunachal Pradesh	1571	2119	2710	3265	3304	3059
Assam	1284	1510	1544	1585	1606	1628
Manipur	1419	1598	1739	1986	1993	—
Meghalaya	1361	1412	1733	1673	1808	1837
Mizoram	1289	2658	4474	7743	—	—
Nagaland	1448	1653	1916	2270	—	—
Tripura	1307	1240	1646	1898	2113	2197
India	1625	1857	2267	2533	2664	2814

Another striking feature of the region's economy is the high percentage of employment in the government sector which accounts for the bulk of the non-development expenditure (Dutta, B., 1994).

Insurgency has created an atmosphere in which financial accountability and internal resource mobilisation have become the main casualties and to the extent insurgency has vitiated the true logic of development.

Monthly per capita expenditure (MPCE) may be accepted as an indicator of standard of living for people, on the basis of minimum calorie intake suggested by Indian Council of Medical Research (ICMR) which should be 2400 for an Indian working (staying) in rural India and 2100 in urban India. This exercise yielded the official or Planning Commission poverty lines (PCE values for 30 days) of rural and urban India at 1973-74 prices as Rs. 49.00 and Rs. 56.64 respectively (Bhattacharya, 1998).

Rural poverty line, in terms of level of consumer expenditure has been defined as an expenditure of Rs. 6400 for a family of 5 at 1983-84 price level which comes to Rs. 106.67 per capita per month in 1983-84 and Rs. 156.25 at 1986-87 prices. Assuming urban poverty level as around 25 per cent higher, the estimated poverty level in Indian urban areas may be set at Rs. 133.34 and Rs. 195.31 for the 1983-84 and 1986-87 prices respectively (Pathak, 1998). It is further estimated as Rs. 275.75 and Rs. 343.00 for the rural and the urban people of NER in the year 1998. Thus an estimated people of 46 per cent in urban India in 1988 were below the poverty line. Corresponding proportion of rural people below poverty line is 52 per cent. Considering the economic condition of NER, the percentage of population below the poverty line is higher in respect of all-India level in 1998.

Dutta and Choudhury (1995) observed that while there was a definite decline in the inequalities in the consumption level of the rural households of NER, there was no such tendency in the urban households. But taking into account both the rural and urban households, it is reasonable to conclude that during the period 1970-71 to 1987-88, the region came closer in the period 1982-83 but after that it diverged to some extent in the period 1986-87 and then in the period 1987-88.

Dutta and Choudhury (1996) noted that the pattern of consumption is most uneven in Assam and is one of the highest among the states of NER though it is considerably less than the average for all India in the rural sector. It can also be pointed out that the poorest section of the society in Assam has been badly affected. It is interesting to note that so far the poorest ten per cent of the rural population is concerned the shares of consumption are relatively better in Manipur and Mizoram than that of their counterpart in NER while for the richest ten per cent, the shares of consumption are relatively better in Assam and Meghalaya (Table 14.11). Coming to the urban sectors of NER, it is worthwhile to mention that the percentage share of expenditure according to poorest ten per cent groups of consumers were found to be better in the state of Nagaland and worst in Assam while for the richest ten per cent of the consumers, the share is relatively better in Assam among the states of NER.

Thus it may be pointed out that the poorest section of the society in Assam has been badly affected. The results reveal that the extent of degree of inequality in the level of living in the states of NER is much more than what is taken to guide some of the decision making elements in connection with resource transfer from Centre to these North-Eastern states particularly in Assam.

There is a need to examine the extent of suicides and levels in different states of NER, as compared to all-India, as a result of different socio-economic conditions. It is observed that highest percentage of suicides occur in the age group 15-29 years (3.76 per cent) followed by 30-44 years age group (2.06%) in the states of NER. This is true for the country also. Region's total suicide is 3.7 per cent as compared to India's total suicides. Regarding the number of suicides, Assam's position is on the top (76.54 per cent) followed by only 17.05 per cent in Tripura (Table 14.6). It is to be noted that maximum number of suicides occur due to illness (11.64 %) followed by unemployment, poverty and drug abuse (6.45 %) and which are observed mainly in the states of Assam and Tripura among the states of NER (Table 14.7). It is striking to note that total number of incidence of crimes (murder, decoity, robbery, theft, riots and others) occurred in the states of NER is 2.93 per cent as compared to India's figure. Among the states of NER Assam's position is on the top (72.83 %) securing 2.13 per cent as compared to all-India level while in other states of NER, the percentages are far below 10 per cent (Table 14.7).

Table 14.6 : Incidence of suicides by age group (1996)

State	By all age group						
	Male	Female	Up to 14	15-29	30-44	45-59	60+
Arunachal Pradesh	38	13	1	15	29	6	—
Assam	1678	814	157	913	804	501	117
Manipur	16	2	—	8	6	4	—
Meghalaya	59	13	2	18	34	12	6
Mizoram	31	3	3	24	6	1	—
Nagaland	26	8	—	16	17	1	—
Tripura	299	256	37	170	148	124	76
India	51206	37035	3404	33925	29138	15393	6381

Source : Statistical Abstract, 1998.

The development of an area is best reflected in the distribution of basic needs like safe drinking water, per capita consumption of electricity, per capita food production etc. (Table 14.8). Regarding the safe drinking water facilities, all the states of NER, except Arunachal Pradesh (70.02 %), are less than the national average (62.30 %). It is striking to note that only 16.21 per cent of total households of Mizoram can drink safe water while water is the life-blood of the environment.

Table 14.7 : Incidence of suicides in N.E. States and India (1996)

	Change in eco. status	Illness	Dowry dispute	Drug abuse	Unemploy-ment	Poverty
Arunachal Pradesh	—	1	—	—	—	—
Assam	30	191	12	24	143	28
Manipur	—	2	—	—	—	—
Meghalaya	—	9	—	—	—	—
Mizoram	—	4	—	5	—	—
Nagaland	—	—	—	1	2	—
Tripura	3	172	19	—	2	5
India	1492	17767	2180	1221	1579	3099

Table 14.8 : Per Capita Grain Production, Consumption of Electricity and Percentage of Households having Electricity, Safe drinking water in N.E. States

	1*	2*	Per capita foodgrain production (in kg.)			3*
	1996-97	1991	1972-73	1980-81	1990-91	1991
Arunachal Pradesh	80.8	70.02	104	207	253	40.85
Assam	107.6	45.86	158	150	154	18.74
Manipur	127.9	38.72	159	205	155	50.92
Meghalaya	134.5	36.16	120	116	87	29.16
Mizoram	127.8	16.21	244	70	118	59.20
Nagaland	88.0	53.37	107	136	160	53.42
Tripura	80.4	37.18	116	196	187	36.93
India	338.5	62.30	172	190	208	42.37

1* per capita consumption of electricity (in Kwh).
2* percentage of households having safe drinking water.
3* percentage of households having electricity.

About the consumption of the electricity it is to be noted that the per capita consumption of electricity is much lower in the states of NER as compared to the country's consumption (338.5 Kwh.). The highest per capita consumption is observed in the state of Meghalaya (134.5 Kwh) and lowest in Tripura (80.4 Kwh).

In the north-eastern hill areas, food production is subject to wide fluctuation due to shifting cultivation. However, during the last two decades, per capita production of food has declined in the states of Assam, Manipur, Meghalaya and Mizoram and are lower than the national average, except Arunachal Pradesh. While the population is rapidly increasing in the states of the region, it is observed that in case of Assam, the per capita food production decreased from 158 Kg in 1972-73 to 154 Kg in 1990-91. The respective figures for Meghalaya are 120 Kg and 87 Kg and for Mizoram 244 Kg and 118 Kg.

Thus, it suggests that in spite of all the resource endowment, agriculture of north-eastern region has remained backward and far behind from the main stream of the country.

The development of an area is best reflected in the quality of life of its people. Quality of life index may be comprised of population growth, literacy rate, female literacy rate, female work participation rate, total work participation rate, dependency ratio, infant mortality rate, public health centres, mean age at marriage, per capita expenditure, sex ratio, urbanisation, per capita net domestic product etc.

Dutta & Roy (1998) observed that urban population significantly affected the literacy rate and per capita net domestic product. Positive significant correlations are observed for LR with PCE, mean age at marriage, per capita net domestic product, female work participation rate while significantly negatively correlated with percentage growth rate. Again, child-women ratio is negatively significantly correlated with sex-ratio, dependency ratio and literacy rate.

Choudhury (1996) working on the National Family Health Survey Data (NFHS) 1992-93 for India suggested that in controlling fertility, schooling of females in the age-group 6-14 plays a vital role.

Forest plays a crucial role in maintaining the ecological balance on the earth. Forests are being cut ruthlessly to make towns, roads etc. which are creating ecological imbalance. Through excessive harnessing of the natural resources has led to rapid warming up of the earth's climate and also endangers extinction. It is observed from the Table 14.9 that among the states of NER, highest deforestation took place in the state of Assam (40 %) followed by Mizoram (25 %) while forest cover gained in the state of Nagaland and Tripura (though the area is very much negligible)after the regeneration of abandoned shifting cultivation during the period 1991-93. On account of deforestation, tempering with nature, uncontrolled grazing in the catchment areas and soil erosion, floods have become a recurring phenomenon in many parts of the region and Assam, in particular. The practice of *Jhum* cultivation has been a major cause of soil degradation, which has serious economic and ecological implications for a region having a predominantly agricultural economy.

Health is a social goal and considered an integral component in overall socio-economic development. The majority of health problems are the

Table 14.9 : Loss/gain in the forest covers in 1993 assessment as compared to 1991 assessment in the N.E. States

State	1991 assessment (Total first cover)	1993 assessment (Total first cover)	Loss due to shifting cultivation	Gain due to degeneration in abandoned shifting cultivation	Net gain (+)/ loss (-) in Areas (sq. kms.)
Arunachal Pradesh	68757	68661	70	—	−70
Assam	24751	24508	165	104	−61
Manipur	17685	17621	28	—	−28
Meghalaya	15875	15769	110	6	−104
Mizoram	18853	18697	256	100	−156
Nagaland	14321	14398	63	90	+27
Tripura	5535	5538	10	15	+5
India	165777	165142	702	315	−387

products of illiteracy, poverty, ignorance, overcrowding, poor environmental conditions and uneven distribution of health, manpower and institutions. It is observed that there are only 4.32 per cent of public health centres in the states of NER (958 in number) as compared to India's figure and only in Assam there are 64 per cent public health centres among the states of NER, while less than 10 per cent are in each of the other states of the region (Table 14.10). The same patterns are observed in case of sub-centres and community health centres. Thus it is a high time to make an effort to increase the number of health centres in backward states of North-Eastern Region so that health problems can be minimized to some extent.

Table 14.10 : No. of Health Centres (As on 31-03-95) and Annual Requirement of Water for Domestic Purposes (Cubic Km.)

	Health Centres			Coverage of problem villages during	Water requirement during (cubic km.)	
	PHC	SC	CHC	1990-91	1991	2001
Arunachal Pradesh	40	203	7	0	0.024	0.029
Assam	619	5180	105	356	0.632	0.883
Manipur	72	420	15	0	0.060	0.074
Meghalaya	88	333	10	406	0.053	0.072
Mizoram	43	244	6	68	0.025	0.035
Nagaland	33	244	5	7	0.036	0.052
Tripura	63	535	10	120	0.080	0.088
India	22156	131902	2377	3031	27.111	33.521

Table 14.11 : Percentage share of consumption by extreme two groups (bottom and top 10 p.c.) of population in rural and urban areas in the N.E. States

State	Rural Bottom 10 p.c.	Rural Top 10 p.c.	Urban Bottom 10 p.c.	Urban Top 10 p.c.
Arunachal Pradesh	3.53	21.93	3.08	24.04
Assam	3.64	21.96	1.35	36.39
Manipur	5.05	17.94	4.58	17.76
Meghalaya	3.26	21.97	3.06	24.61
Mizoram	5.11	16.76	4.17	17.95
Nagaland	—	—	6.18	16.54
Tripura	3.92	20.52	3.96	20.16
India	2.85	25.16	2.01	29.84

It has been observed that there is no problem village in Arunachal Pradesh and Manipur regarding supply of drinking water. While number of problem villages are found in Meghalaya (42.42 %), Assam (37.2 %) and Tripura (12.5 %) among the states of NER. However, almost one-third problem villages of India (3032) are found in states of North-Eastern Region. A look at the table, it is observed that the maximum amount of water is required in the states of Assam among the states of NER, which is approximately 2.33 per cent as compared to India's requirement in 1991 and the figure (0.883 Cubic Km.) will rise to 2.63 per cent in 2001. However, there is an increasing trend of water requirement in 2001 over 1991. Conservation of water is an important aspect in this regard. We, the people of N.E. India should take active step for the management of water for the maintenance of the standard of water quality.

Environment is the sum total of social, biological, physical and chemical factors which compose the surroundings of men. Man has played a very important part in shaping his environment. Man himself is responsible for degrading the quality of his environment ever since he appeared in this earth.

Fig 14.1 reveals the complex relationships among population growth, poverty, health and environmental hazards. Population explosion in N.E. India has led to health hazard as well as environmental imbalance. The root cause of human health hazard is the improper disposal of sewage and wastes. Slum dwellings and unhygienic conditions may lead to the spread of disease causing micro-organisms. The microbial pathogens in this concern mainly include viruses, fungi and bacteria. However poverty is an important factor for health hazard which results in the development of frustration. Again frustration develops due to unemployment and poverty which is the consequence of food shortage. Now-a-days, drug abuse is a burning problem in the North-Eastern states of India which is a result of frustration.

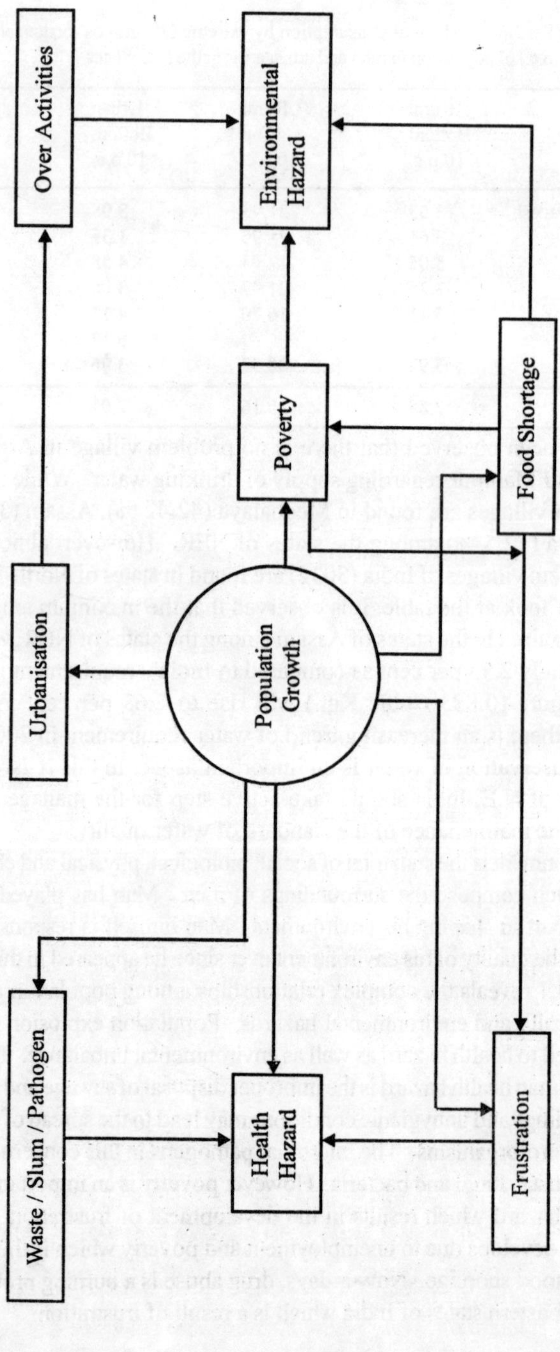

Fig. 14.1 : Population Growth and Socio-economic Crisis

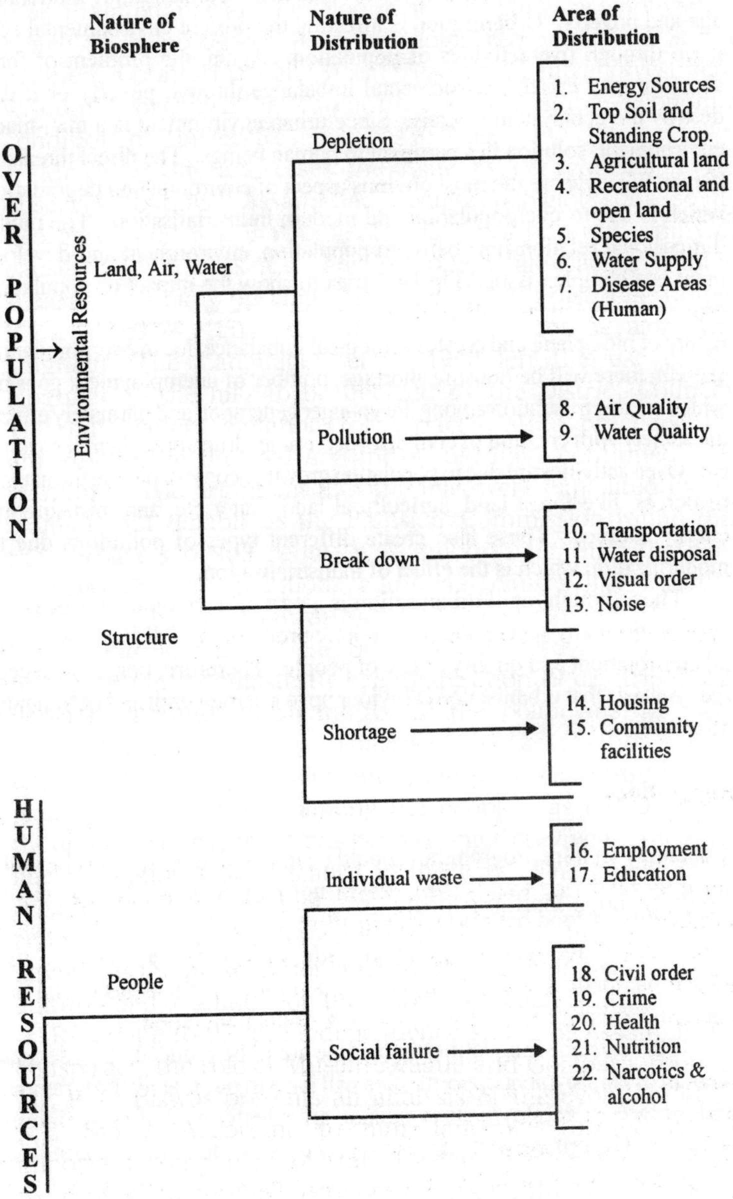

Fig. 14.2 : Impact of over population on environment

Environmental imbalance may be resulted from urbanisation, food shortage and poverty. Urbanisation is affecting the present environmental scenario through overactivities of population. Again, the problem of food shortage may create environmental imbalance through poverty or it can destroy the eco-system directly. Since urban environment is a man-made environment, solution lies pertinent to human beings. The direct threats to human life style are the most obvious aspect of environmental degradation which is due to overpopulation and modern industrialisation. The multi-dimensional relationships between population, environment and development is a complex issue. Fig 14.2 tries to show the impact of population growth on society as well as on environment. Overpopulation affects the nature of bio-sphere and creates ecological imbalance due to overpopulation growth, there will be housing shortage, number of unemployment goes up which creates frustration among the younger generation and ultimately effects the society with creation of civil disorder, crime, drug abuse, health hazards etc. Over-activities are due to population growth, people depleting the natural resources, like forest land, agricultural land, water etc. and misusing the energy sources. These also create different types of pollutions due to modernization which is the effect of industrialisation.

Thus, though rapid urbanisation is a part of development process, it accelerates many severe socio-economic problems and disturbs the overall environment and quality of life of people. Therefore, one must accept the synthesis that urbanisation is saviour up to a certain limit and detrimental after without check to it.

Suggestions

The family welfare programmes should be initiated honestly and sincerely since by revolving family size, it will not only increase the per capita availability of food but also result in all-round facilities including health care. The Government should provide various social services like education, medical aid, labour welfare and other services for social and economic security of the weaker section of the population.

If the extreme inequalities in income are to be reduced, the adequate amount of employment opportunities will have to be created. Programmes and projects of employment expansion are a better way of redistributing incomes. The criteria of backwardness should be the economic condition of a person rather than his caste, language, tribe or area so that all the poor people irrespective of caste, language, tribe etc. should have equal opportunity to get education, training and employment. Anti-poverty schemes such as the food for work programme, employment guarantee schemes, other income guaranteeing plans and developmental activities should be initiated honestly without any vertical or horizontal interference.

The Government should take positive interest in upgrading the status of female by giving opportunity for their education, employment and security.

Environmental Awareness Programmes at all levels should be sponsored by governmental and non-governmental agencies engaged in environment development. Environmental awareness should be strengthened through formal and non-formal education.

It is necessary to recast the whole urbanisation process and adopt the urban environment policy in such a way that urbanisation would urge to create environmental balance. Open burning of used raw material bags beeds to be stopped as it causes air pollution.

Government should establish the requisite institutional mechanism and enabling environment at all levels of society to ensure that population factors are appropriately addressed within the decision making and administrative process of all government agencies responsible for economic, environment and social policies and programmes.

Investment in human resource development in accordance with national policy must be given priority in population and development strategies and budgets, at all levels, with programmes specifically directed at increased access to information, education, skill development, all types of employment opportunities through the promotion of sustained economic growth within the context of sustainable development in developing countries.

REFERENCES

APRET (1998) : "Population Issues - II" Three contributions, Applied Population Research Trust, Bangalore.

Bhattacharya, N. (1998) : "On Level of Living Surveys in India", *Presidential Address, 85th Indian Science Congress Association, Section of Statistics,* 1998.

Choudhury, H. (1996) : NFHS Findings on Nuptiality Pattern and Policy Implications for the States Meghalaya, Mizoram and Tripura based on National Family Health Survey (NFHS) Results" - *Paper presented in the Regional Seminar on Dissemination of findings NFHS reports for the NE States,* Nov. 27-29, Guwahati, 1996.

Dutta, B.B. (1994) : "Insurgency and Economic Development in India's North East" in *India's North East : The Process of Change and Development,* B.R. Publishing, Delhi.

Dutta P.C. & Choudhury, H. : "Per Capita Household Consumption Inequalities in the North Eastern Region of India", *Indian Journal of Regional Science,* Vol. 27, Nos. 1 & 2.

Dutta, P.C. (1996) : "Quality Variation of Some Food Items of Consumption in the North Eastern Region (NER)", *IJRS Vol. 28 No. 1.*

Dutta P.C. & Choudhury, H. (1996) : "A note on Inter State Variation in Per Capita Non-Food Household Items of Consumption in the North East India", *IJRS,* Vol. 28, No. 2.

Dutta P.C. & Pradhan, B.C. (1998) : "Problems of Community Integration in Small Towns of Barak Valley Districts of Assam — Case Study of Lala Town" in *Urban Development in North East India : Potentiality and Problems.* Ed. B. Dutta Roy, A.K. Neog & H.K. Mazhari, Reliance Publishing House, New Delhi.

Dutta, P.C. & Roy, N. (1998) : "Socio-Economic Development of North East India with Special Reference to the Problems of Urbanisation", *Paper presented and published in the Abstract of Seminar on Environmental Problems in North East India,* 6th and 7th Nov., 1998, Assam University, Silchar.

Madhab, Jayanta (1999) : "North East : Crisis of Identity, Security and Underdevelopment", *Economic and Political Weekly, Vol. 34, No. 1,* Feb. 6-12.

Pathak, C.R. (1998) : "Urbanisation and Urban Poverty in Third World Countries : A Case Study of India", in *Essays on Regional Science, Regional Development and Planning,* Vol. II, *RSAI,* Calcutta.

Patil, S.Y. (1998) : "Environmental Impact on Urbanisation in India" in *Essays on Regional Science, Regional Development and Planning,* Vol. II, *RSAI,* Calcutta-91.

Procharopouclus, G. (1994) : "Returns to Investment in Education : A Global Update" *World Development,* pp. 1325-43.

Singh, U.K. & Sudharshan, K.N. (1996) : "Population Education" DPH Education Series, Discovery Publishing House, New Delhi.

15

POPULATION GROWTH AND DEMOGRAPHIC BALANCE IN THE NORTH-EAST IN THE THRESHOLD OF THE NEW MILLENNIUM

Kailash Sarma

We know that population growth is the most dynamic factor operating in an economy and the other factors only synchronise with it. North-East India is a small but significant part of the country comprising only 7.77 per cent area of the whole country. The total land area of the country and of the constituent states of North-East is given below :

Table 15.1 : Land Area of the North-East States and of the country

States		Area in Sq. Km.	Percentage to total of the Country
1.	Arunachal Pradesh	83578	2.55
2.	Assam	78523	2.39
3.	Manipur	22356	0.68
4.	Meghalaya	22489	0.69
5.	Mizoram	21087	0.64
6.	Nagaland	16527	0.50
7.	Tripura	10477	0.32
8.	N.E. India	255039	7.77
	India	3280483	100.00

Source : India, 1974.

According to 1991 Census, North-East Region has 315.47 lakh of population, which represents 8.73 per cent of the total population of the country.

Before discussing the trend in population growth of the North-East Region in the recent past and the projected pupulation growth in the near future, we should have to discuss and analyse the correlation of population growth and demographic balance of an economy either at the national level or at the state level.

Demographic balance could not be understood in the sense of ecological balance as in between the man and the nature. Ecological balance between the two encourages a healthy growth of the people and of the natural kingdom without creating any induced natural hazards, on the other hand demographic balance does mean a balance in between the different ethnic, religious or linguistic or culture groups of people so as to have an atmosphere of mutual confidence interdependence without any fear or force. This balance between different groups of people is seen to be disturbed due to various reasons. Some may be political in nature, some are religious fundamentalism, and still some are cultural or linguistic chauvinism. This tendency has been enforced in recent years due to demographic empowerment or open-endedness of our national borders.

In a multi-community country like India, every community tries not only to preserve its own identity but also to enrich itself to glorify it as far as it can. In a democratic set-up of such a multi-community nation, the majority has the automatic right to rule over the minorities, though often constitutional safeguards are at the same time provided with.

The tendency to enrich and empower their community strength is only possible through increasing the numerical strength of the community. For this they adopt a policy of high birth rate and low death rate and also if possible, encourage migration of their community brethren from across the borders. Sometimes the leaders of the community are seen misusing their enumerating power at the time of census operation. It is alleged that such practices are adopted in the last census 1991 in certain places by certain communities in Assam.

Thus we see a very close but negative correlation between demography and democracy. As democracy is a game of numbers and demography itself is the science of numbers of population, so all minority groups try to strengthen their respective position by increasing their numbers. So the growth of population should be higher than that of the majorities. So a time comes when the existing balance in between the different groups of people in the country or the region is disturbed. The very law of demography could not be seen applied in such an economy. This trend in population growth creates innumerable social, economic, political and even cultural problems in the society. Peace and tranquility sometimes abruptly go to the backseat and a turmoil in between the peoples is created. Social tension arises and ultimately terrorism shows its ugly head.

If the rate of growth of population of all sections of the society remains the same demographic balance is not feared disturbed. And once it is disturbed, it initiates the atomosphere for which the very population policy of a small family cannot be implemented. If one section of the society is advocating for a small family at one time it feels and sees that a death knell is expected to befall on it at the macrolevel. Without any coercion and strong lucrative inducement, all the sections cannot be expected to practise the family planning measures with equal vigour. Rather when there is some ulterior motive like religious expansion, political domination or cultural suzerainty, such a population policy has to be kept in cold storage. Particularly it so happens when the government is seen to be composed of various factions of the society without much political will and principle.

For these reasons, we have realised that the demographic balance that prevailed at one time in between the different groups of people — ethnic, religious, cultural or linguistic in the North-East could not expected to be in the coming future.

The North-East is only geographically a compact area though demographically heterogeneous. Just after the partition of the country nay after the partition of Bengal in 1904, the demographic balance has been significantly disturbed. Large number of people of different religious groups speaking a different language migrated to this part of the country. If the proportion of the groups migrating to the region had been also the same, then also balance would have not been disturbed. But unfortunately that did not take place.

Let us see how the growth rates of total population and of tribal population differed at different periods of time. During 1951-61 total population increased by 3.46 per cent per annum against 22.90 per cent of tribal population. In 1991 total population growth rate has reduced to 2.46 per cent against an increased rate of growth of tribal population by 32.16 per cent. During this perod total population in the Region has increased from 1,45,01,000 in absolute term in 1961, which increased to 3,15,47,314 in 1991. Against this tribal population has increased from 33,20,855 in 1961 to 81,42,626 in 1991. For this reason tribal population percentage has increased from 22.9 per cent to 25.81 per cent of the total population of the North-East. This proportion of tribal population is expected to reach 26.71 per cent in 2001 and 37.87 per cent in 2011. The projected population of the N.E. Region is expected to be 3,91,20,607 in 2001 and 4,75,83,454 in 2011. We have also projected the total and tribal population of the seven constituent states and they are presented in Table 15.2 below :

Table 15.2 : Total population and tribal population in the N.E. States 1961, 1991, 2001 and 2011 (Projected)

States	Category of Population	1961	1991	2001 Projected	2011 Projected
Arunachal Pradesh	All	337000	864558	1160237	1519910
	Tribal	298167	550351	702872	873948
Assam	All	11144785	22414322	26740286	31740719
	Tribal	1164641	28714441	3412060	4342130
Manipur	All	780000	1837149	2360736	2995774
	Tribal	249049	632173	748353	7541540
Meghalaya	All	770000	1774778	2346256	3094712
	Tribal	644167	1617927	2017780	2671046
Mizoram	All	266063	689756	909098	1130918
	Tribal	261014	653565	863279	1074372
Nagaland	All	369000	1209546	1903825	2084295
	Tribal	343697	1060822	1582079	1796662
Tripura	All	1142000	2757205	3700169	4947126
	Tribal	360070	853345	1123001	1491558
N.E.India	All	14501000	31547314	39120607	47583454
	Tribal	3320855	8142626	10449424	17991256
%of Tribals	To All Pop.	(22.90)	(25.81)	(26.71)	(37.87)

Sources : 1. Demographic and Economic Profiles for the North-East India for 1961 data Population Totals : 1991 census for 1991 data.

2. For data 2001 and 2011, graphically projected population.

This imbalance is seen due to abnormal rise in the growth of population particularly among the tribals. Rate of growth of tribal population is seen much higher in all the hill states of the N.E. India though the literacy percentage is seen much higher even more than 90 per cent. Even in Assam the growth rate of the tribal population is seen much higher than that of the general people particularly since 1971.

The other two significant factors disturbing the population balance are religions and languages spoken by each cultural segment of the population. So let us have at first a peep into the religious composition of population of the North-East.

Table 15.3 : Religious Composition of Population in India since 1951

(In %)

Year	Hindu	Muslim	Christian	Others
1951	84.98	9.91	2.35	2.76
1961	83.50	10.7	2.44	3.36
1971	82.72	11.20	2.59	3.49
1991	82.00	12.12	2.34	3.54

Source : North East India, R. Gopalkrishnan — 1995.

Census of India : Table No. 2.3 census data outline through internet.

The above data of religious composition of population in the country since 1951 show the trend of change of different religious groups in the country and it proves what we have expressed earlier in this chapter. Hindu population has been decreased significantly in proportion during this period 1951-1991, while Muslim population proportion has been seen increased continuously from 9.91 per cent to 12.12 per cent. The Christian population proportion has also been seen slightly decreased. For this reason we see an ominous sign of imbalance rising its ugly head here and there in the country. If this trend continues in the coming future, we can expect that the Hindu population will rise at a declining rate limiting the proportion at 80.99 per cent in 2011, Muslim population, at a rising rate, limiting it at 13.12 per cent and the Christian population, at 2.91 per cent, other religious groups like Sikh, Buddhist, Jains etc. are expected to rise at a rate of 2.98 per cent by that time.

The situation in the North-East is expected to be slightly different because the religious composition of population in it is seen quite different in the past. The following Table 15.4 will speak about it.

Table 15.4 : Religious Composition of Population in N.E. since 1951

(In %)

Year	Hindu	Muslim	Christian	Others
1951	65.61	20.88	6.34	7.17
1971	58.51	19.18	8.68	13.63
1991	60.92	21.56	12.25	3.95

Source : As of Table-15.3

Hindu population here constitutes only even less than three-fifths and it is seen continuously falling through the decades from 65.61 per cent in 1951 to 58.51 per cent in 1971. Of course in 1991 we have seen a rising trend to reach 60.92 per cent. If this trend of falling and rising continues, it is expected that by 2011 Hindu population will only constitute 59.44 per cent. But the Muslims have shown a falling rate during the decade 1951-61 perhaps because of the impact of partition of the country. But thereafter it shows a rising trend during 1971-1991 to reach 21.56 per cent. By projection on these data base it is expected to rise at a slightly lowering rate to reach 21.41 per cent. But the Christian population in the region has been seen rising at a very high speed indicating that at normal growth rate population could not subscribe to this. Conversion in the hilly region is going on unabated for which the proportion of others in the region seen decreased significantly from 13.63 in 1971 to 3.95 in 1991, while Christian population increasing from 6.34 per cent in 1951 to 12.25

per cent in 1991. If this trend continues and the people of other communities like the traditional animists are converted to Christianity being experienced no resistance from the neighbours, thereby up to 2011 Christian population will reach tallying position of 15.21 per cent of the total population of the region. The following Table 15.5 presents the proportion of different religious communities in the different constituent states of the North-East.

Table 15.5 : Religions composition of population of the North-Eastern States (in %)

States	Year	Hindu	Muslim	Christians	Others
Arunachal	1951	—	—	—	—
Pradesh	1971	21.99	0.18	0.79	77.09
	1991	37.04	1.38	10.29	51.29
Assam	1951	72.08	24.68	2.00	1.24
	1971	72.51	24.96	2.61	0.32
	1991	67.13	28.43	3.32	1.12
Manipur	1951	60.00	6.44	11.89	21.59
	1971	58.97	6.11	26.03	8.39
	1991	57.67	7.27	34.11	0.95
Meghalaya	1951	12.12	2.30	29.66	53.96
	1971	18.50	2.60	49.95	25.89
	1991	14.07	3.46	64.58	27.88
Mizoram	1951	3.30	0.07	90.51	6.21
	1971	6.39	0.57	86.08	6.96
	1991	5.05	0.66	85.73	8.56
Nagaland	1951	4.70	0.24	46.05	49.63
	1971	11.43	0.58	66.76	21.23
	1991	10.12	1.71	87.47	0.70
Tripura	1951	75.92	21.43	0.82	1.83
	1971	89.55	6.08	1.01	2.76
	1991	86.50	7.13	1.68	4.72

Sources : Census of India - 1951, 1971, 1991.
North-East India — R. Gopal Krishna - Har Ananda' 1995.
India - 1990, 1994.

From the above table, it has become evident that all the units are not equally affected by the growth of population of different religious groups. Mizoram has not been seen affected by this trend. Tripura has suffered seriously just after independence, but thereafter the trend has become non-effective. Considering the proportions of population Assam is seen not affected so much from the growth, but if we consider the absolute figures, the fear of an imbalance is looming large on the sky of the state. But in Arunachal Pradesh, Manipur, Meghalaya and Nagaland population balance has already been disturbed of course, the sufferance has been at the cost of the 'other' category.

On the basis of the trend shown in the above table we can project out what would be the population proportions belonging to the different religious groups.

Table 15.6 : Projected population proportions of religious groups in the constituent states of North-East India in 2011

States	Proportions and absolute no. of population					
	Hindus		Muslims		Christians	
	Population	%	Population	%	Population	%
Arunachal	694159 (117.6)	46.60	30398 (154.8)	2	88963 (133.5)	13.67
Assam	21065125 (40)	59.82	9493649 (27.3)	29.19	1022083 (37.3)	3.22
Manipur	1701600 (158.5)	56.80	228578 (71.1)	7.63	1049120 (67.4)	35.02
Meghalaya	402085 (39.0)	12.99	12255 (99.6)	3.74	2057983 (79.6)	66.50
Mizoram	45237 (29.9)	4.00	9952 (118.6)	0.88	969536 (63.3)	85.73
Nagaland	193839 (58.3)	9.30	54608 (164.00)	2.62	109826 (195.3)	87.50
Tripura	4170364 (16.5)	84.42	383402 (95.0)	7.75	1823758 (137.1)	2.22
N.E. India	28283409 (47.2)	59.44	10188158 (31.4)	21.41	7240078 (68.3)	15.21

Note : Figures within brackets are growth rate over 1991 population.
Source : As of Table 15.5.

From Table 15.6 we see that in 2011 projected population of different religious groups will make a significant change in the different constituent states. As is in the past, Hindu population will still constitute the majority of the population in the whole of North-East as well as in Assam and Tripura. Muslim population will still make it the second majority segment of population in the North-East but it will now be more significant. It will remain so in Assam and Tripura consolidating its position further. Christian population in the north-eastern states occupies a special position, particularly in the hill states of the Region, namely Meghalaya, Mizoram, and Nagaland where they constitute more than 66 per cent of the state's population. But if we see the trend of its growth since 1951 we see that at the time or just after independence, proportion of Christian population in states like Meghalaya, Nagaland and Manipur was significantly less than what it has been in the 1991 census period; of course, in Mizoram there has been an opposite trend in its growth. We expect that in 2011, there might be a slight change in the trend as there is already an anti-estab-lishment mood of the locality or a mood to preserve the traditionality and so the rate of growth of population is expected to be slightly different at the time of census in 2011.

Further it is seen from the same Table 15.6 that the growth rate of population in 2011 over 1991 for different religious groups of people is not of uniform nature. In Arunachal Pradesh, Manipur and Nagaland the rate of growth of the Hindus is much higher even than the normal, while in Tripura it is seen to be abnormally low. In the rest it is of normal nature. For the Muslims this rate for the North-East though expected to be even less than the normal, is seen much higher in most of the states. For the Christians this rate is seen in every state higher except in Assam. In Nagaland, Tripura and Arunachal Pradesh it is very high, higher than 6.7 per annum. So it seems that this higher rate in the region as a whole may help in the growth potential of population imbalance.

The North-East India is said to be the home of a very large number of languages like the Assamese, Bengali, Bodo/Boro, Manipuri, Khasi, Tripuri, Garo, Lushai/Mizo, Mishing, Karbi, Ao, Sema, Kanyak, Thado, Tangkul, Dimasa, Hmar, Tiwa, Hindi, Nepali, Bishnupuriya, Rabha, Nissi/Daffla, Lakher. Of these languages Assamese, Bengali, Hindi, Nepali and Manipuri are scheduled languages, while all others are non-scheduled. Generally language is not so strong a factor as religion is creating disharmony in a region. But in the North-East the past is not happy at least during the British period when the then Government superimposed Bengali over some parts of the region as the administrative language. Since that time the local people are very sincere in preserving their own identity of cultural and linguistic orgin. And so some disharmonic concords are seen playing in recent times in between the different cultural groups like the Bodos, the Karbis, the Hmars, the Nagas etc. We are therefore showing the comparative linguistic position of different language groups here.

Table 15.7 : Linguistic Composition of the population of the North-East in 1971 and 1991

Languages	1971*	1991
Assamese	8904917 (45.63)	12958088 (41.08)
Bengali	2882039 (14.77)	4696326 (14.89)
Bodo/Boro	533713 (2.73)	1184569 (3.75)
Manipuri	87167 *	1110134 (3.52)
Khasi	—	879192 (2.79)
Tripuri	—	647847 (2.05)
Garo	—	547690 (1.76)
Lushai/Mizo	—	518099 (1.64)

Source : Census of India, Statement No. 3, Paper 1 of 1997 Language, received through Internet.

Note : * 1971 Census Data are for Assam alone which included Mizo hills also.

Table 15.7 is not found complete by itself but yet it is helpful to us. It shows that the Assamese speaking population is decreasing in proportion over the years 1971-1991, while Bengali and Bodo speaking people are increasing in proportion. It is doubted that in the coming century, this trend will continue and may aggravate the situation. This may be so when a minor linguistic group choses to mention in the census schedule that their mother tongue is not Assamese but their own dialect. Of course there may be another alignment in the form of using Assamese in a different form like Nagamese, Arunachalese, as the *lingua franca* in between different dialects speaking sections of Nagaland and Aruanchal Pradesh. But it may be said that conversion of particular language speaking people to another is not so easy as it is in case of religion. So we do not think it necessary to analyse the language data in a more detailed way as such division could not create any further imbalance in the region further.

In conclusion, therefore, we may say that the new millennium is to be really a challenge to the people of the North-East. Growth rate of population, no doubt, would perhaps remain almost constant or even it may be reduced to a certain extent. But the relative position of the different ethnic or religious groups would undergo a change even in the early part of the century. Religio-political consideration, therefore, may cause some sort of anxiety for which precaution is very much essential. We appeal, therefore, to all concerned to come to the negotiation table to arrive at a consensus, so that they could maintain the original balance in between themselves. Tolerance, mutual understanding, patriotism, cooperation in nation building activities, growth of spiritual ideas among the people all will help in maintaining the balance between the people.

16

NON-GOVERNMENTAL ORGANISATIONS AND SOCIAL DEVELOPMENT : A Critique

B. J. Deb

There can be no dispute about the fact that Non-Governmental Organisations (NGOs) have come to occupy focus of attention in social, economic and political landscapes across the globe. As a matter of fact, NGO discourse has gained currency the world over filled with notions of people's involvement, empowerment, greater representation of the poor and dispossessed and more equitable access to scarce resources. Indeed the emergence of NGOs as a possible alternative paradigm of social change and development represents a new hope in the much expected transformation of the notion of community participation. That participatory approach is capable of delivering the goods as compared to the prescriptive one is now an unassailable fact, amply demonstrated in diverse fields which include environment, disaster management, empowerment, rural development, human rights, market economy, education, social reforms, philanthropy and even political mobilization.[1] No wonder it is argued that the plurality of interests and forms of resistance associated with NGOs also go a long way in allowing them a distinct space in civil society not merely as platform of social dissent but as harbinger of change in the new liberalised economic environment.[2]

NGOs today cover a wide spectrum of organizations which include voluntary organizations, non-profit associations, new social-movement organizations, people's organizations, membership organizations, community associations, cooperatives, church groups, trade unions, environmental groups, consumer associations, women's groups, credit unions and peasant leagues. At the same time, there are also large international organizations like Amnesty International, OXFAM and Friends of the Earth.

In fact, most of the NGOs function within the boundaries set up by the state. That is why the questions of institutional legitimacy and autonomy come to the forefront of discussion. As is well known, voluntarism distinguishes NGOs from the Government and commercial sectors. Significantly, NGOs are different from state and market institutions which are motivated by the need for social coercion and profit respectively. In the words of Paul Streeten, by NGOs we refer to voluntary private associations that mobilize the commitment and enthusiasm of volunteers to the objectives of relieving suffering and of promoting development.[3] It has been rightly said that the incorporation of voluntarism into NGO programmes helps make them sustainable.

Undoubtedly, NGOs function within the boundaries set by the state and are governed by various laws and regulations. Although NGOs are non-profit organizations, recent tendencies reveal that some of them function as for-profit bodies and the traditional distinction between non-profit and for-profit may get blurred in the wake of market oriented economic reforms and ever-increasing collaboration between NGOs and international agencies.

In the recent decades, NGOs have come to occupy a distinct space in civil society in both developed and developing countries around the world. The term NGO for the first time used in the U.N. forum in 1949 has also acquired magical legitimacy based upon certain claim maintained by its protagonists which however may or may not hold true in countries where constraints to social and human development obviously nullify the very idea of alternative development. Nevertheless, the fact remains that with the idea of NGO participation and input as a means of ensuring transformation of the civil society in certain socially desirable fields, the space between the state and its citizens continues to gain ground holding out hopes, however little it may be to the disillusioned poor, remote and marginalised communities.[4]

Against this background, it is held that the increasing activism of NGO symbolises a break from the conventional model of development which assigned primary responsibility to the state and the markets. One must at the same time guard against the tall claim of Lester Salmon that NGOs may constitute the significant economic and social development of the twentieth century. It is however true that new social movements arose largely from NGO activism, although hasty conclusion is drawn signifying the emergence of alternative paradigm of social change as if it could be on a self-propelled and self-sustaining force. Admittedly the demise of the vanguardist role of the working class is not disputed but it is precisely the failure of the political parties and trade unions in delivering the goods that have induced people in developing countries to turn around NGOs for signalling dissent and resistance. It cannot be ignored that people's disenchantment against the non-performing role of the political parties often gets directed against the government. The euphoria apart, the principal aim of the NGOs in developing countries is to disseminate information about development inputs, to contribute to the reduction of human sufferings and above all to raise the level of awareness in socially desirable fields.[5]

In general, NGO activities are not directed as such against dominant policy and political regimes. In fact, just as the success of NGOs could be attributed to positive attitude of the state towards their contributory role, their failure to address issues of concern could arise from their autonomy fetish. Indeed, responsiveness is no coverage for unaccountability whether social or financial. The comparative advantage enjoyed by the NGOs calls for their adequate linkages with state and market institutions. Without evolving a mechanism of checks and balance between them the mere cry of autonomy may turn out to be self-defeating.[6] As a matter of fact as NGOs become more active in developmental efforts the existing laws, inadequate as they are, ought to be streamlined to ensure social and financial accountability in particular. Functional autonomy is however necessary to prevent governmental interference and inroads of political parties.

There can however be no dispute about the rationale of bottom-up approach for spreading the fruits of development and it is here the NGOs are capable of making a dent in view of their organizational priorities and procedural flexibilities. This is how NGOs have acquired popular legitimacy but in developing countries their role is still confined to peripheral areas. Consequently, state despite serving dominant interests has not lost the confidence of the masses, particularly poor people as is made out to be. Despite lopsided results, the developmental and welfare goals of the state remains undisputed. Eventually, the NGOs can go not further than supplementing and not supplanting developmental priorities. The political economy of developing countries is full of contradictions and paradoxes which also limit the scope of NGO participation. While NGOs are not involved as such in ideological polemics, they have taken in their strides the emerging consensus arising out of the widespread criticism of top-down or trickle-down model of growth from both neo-classical economists and neo-Marxists. Ideological shortcomings and failures notwithstanding the state abdication of socio-economic responsibility is ruled out and new challenges from globalization have further complicated the situation inasmuch as the perennial issues of inequality, deprivation and exploitation need to be addressed. No doubt state failure looms large and civic society is poised for expansion against the backdrop of eternal human urge for freedom but the fact remains that apart from democratization of state power no alternative seems conceivable.

It hardly needs any reiteration that the apparent advantages of NGOs are many. Apart from their sensitivity to local conditions, NGO activism stands for participatory approaches for strengthening membership associations' claims on the state. Group-based initiatives however constitute the key to the success of the NGOs. They operate at low costs and their emphasis on self-help and bottom-up programmes makes them people-oriented as opposed to bureaucratic state activities. Further, by providing a venue for discussion and debate around issues of poverty, equality, literacy, environment, empowerment and access to credit the NGOs in developing countries may indirectly play a key role in the struggle for democracy.

Be that as it may, some of the other claimed advantages may not turn out to be true. Frequently they do not reach the poorest segment of the population in several developing countries. Admittedly, NGOs are predominantly urban phenomenon and they serve particular interests. Besides many organisations are clearly elitist even if this takes the form of 'consciousness raising' of the poor. Further erosion of societal values tends to affect the goals of the NGOs as their personnel coming as they do from the unemployed sector of the economy are also a part and parcel of the society. In addition, NGOs are incapable of broad-based sustainable social change. Nor are they well-equipped to ignite the social mobilization of the oppressed. The very lack of coordinated approach among the NGOs even at the regional level, not to speak of the state or national level, goes to dismantle much of their tall claims. In ideal situation community participation could indeed become the supplementary hub of development efforts if decentralization of power through grassroot organisations could be institutionalised with empowerment at desirable level. Since that did not happen disenchantment of the people in developing countries in the form of opposition to the state policies has found expression in NGO activism and rhetoric, although the very fact of their dependence on state financing brings to the focus the limits of this new found frontier. Decentralization and participation should cease to be slogans and instead ignite involvement of the masses in real terms.

NOTES

1. For details one can profitably make use of
   (i) *Year Book of International Associations* : Brussels, Union of International Association, 1999-2000.
   (ii) United Nations Development Programme, *Human Development Report,* 1999; New York, Oxford University Press, 1999.
   (iii) Lester Salmon, "The Rise of Non-Profit Sector", Foreign Affairs, 73(4): 34, 1994.
2. Shelley Feldman, "NGOs and Civil Society" : (Un)stated Contradictions, *The Annals,* AAPSS, 554, November 1997, pp. 46-65.
   In the case of India, "many of the more radical social movements and organisations of dissent and protest against the government have.... adopted a voluntary and non-party, non-government form. Although it is hard to echo the view this had led to a depoliticization of this challenge against poverty, inequality and social injustice; yet there can be no doubt that NGO format has acquired legitimacy." Rajni Kothari, "NGOs : the State and World Capitalism", *Economic and Political Weekly,* 13 Dec., 1986, p. 2180.
3. Paul Streeten, Non-governmental Organisations and Development, *The Annals,* AAPSS, 554, Nov. 1997, pp. 193-210.
4. Shelley Feldman, n. 2.
5. See Hernando de Soto, *The Other Path : The Invisible Revolution in the Third World.* New York : Harper & Row, 1989. The key role played by NGOs in Bangladesh in the struggle for democracy is indeed noteworthy as it provided vitality to the concept of civil society within the development paradigm.
6. At one time it was argued that NGO autonomy may be protected and nurtured by consciously avoiding institutional linkages within state and market institutions (Walter Fernandes, *Voluntary Action and Government Control,* New Delhi, Indian Social Science Institute, 1981).
   For current understanding see Bishwapriya Sanyal, NGO's Self-defeating Quest for Autonomy, *The Annals,* 554, November 1997.

17

TOWARDS A SENSIBLE PARTICIPATION OF PEOPLE

D. N. Chakravarty

Sense of participation in functions like social, religious and other activities is already prevalent among the village people of NE states and for that matter in the nation as a whole. What is new is our level of perception of this paradigm and weakness in approach for effective participation. There is still widespread neglect of protective social security and economic development for unorganized sector which is based on assumption that poors are so numerous that a comprehensive cover for them will be financially unviable. This attitude that believe nothing can be done is the result of the fact that nobody wants to upset the present situation. In reality it is the lack of will and not of fund. So even after five decades of anti-poverty programme neither poverty nor the associated problems like social exclusion, gender discrimination, education and health care could be solved. The ratio of living standards between richest and poorest countries in the world was about 3:1 in 1820 which have risen to 11:1 in 1913, 35:1 in 1950 and now it is more than 70:1. The UN declared 1996 as the International year for Eradication of poverty followed by World summit which suggested the earlier decade as the International Decade for the Eradication of Poverty. But no concrete result has been observed. Instead there is a rising revolution of frustration and helplessness in most areas. India's Human Development Index rank is 139 out of total 174 countries. Such social indicator places India in a dismal position. People have become distrustful of the abilities of the government agencies and public institutions to deliver good governance. Trust in the bureaucracy (37%) and police (28%) are particularly low. On the other hand, rapid and unprecedented change in all sections of our society and economy, created obsolescence in plans, capacities and institutions at an unprecedented rate.

Recent study conducted by the society for Participatory Research in

Asia (PRIA) revealed that Indian citizens are fed up with the treatment given out by government. They no longer want to be mere beneficiaries of schemes designed and imposed on them. Rather they want to be well read citizens who can significantly contribute to an ever-deepening democracy and development. In political manifesto real needs and demands of people are not echoed in newspapers. The UNDP report on Human Development (1993) refer to an important urge among the people to participate in the events and processes that shape their lives.

Eradication of poverty is an ethical, social, political and economic imperative of mankind. A successful nation has three attributes — politically it is free and democratic, economically it is prosperous and equitable, and socially it is peaceful and cohesive. India scores high in political front but low in economic front. How it fairs in the social front needs to be explored in greater depths. According to the UN, social development is to fulfil the great capacity of social system, social structure, institutions, services and policy to utilize resource to generate favourable changes in the level of living. The UN separated Social Development from Economic Development in 1950. Earlier Social Development was perceived as economic growth. Later economists also realised the importance of human factors, which were neglected in economic development. Social development is much vaster than economic development.

The satisfaction of human needs and aspirations is the major objective of development. The essential needs of majority of our people like food, clothing, shelter, jobs etc., are not satisfied beyond basic levels. So a society has to compromise its ability in many ways to meet the essential needs. Large sections of the population are marginalised due to ill-conceived development priorities. Major sections of our community have remained uneffected by modern, high energy inputs and technology. A country with endemic condition of poverty and inequality is always prone to ecological and other crisis which are adverse to sustainable development. Sustainable development requires meeting the essential needs of all citizens and extending all opportunities to satisfy their aspirations for a better life. Sustainable development is a series of compromises. It is increasingly realised that the basic weakness of our comprehension is undertaking the need to integrate ecological sciences with sociological sciences and have our action oriented on participatory mode.

Community input in the form of systematic arrangement for participation of people in policy making and for regular feedback may help in decision making process at different levels. The community could utilize natural resources as well as human and other social capitals (such as enthusiasm, ability and energy of the youths and women) for their development which otherwise might remain unused. It is also desirable and imperative that the intended beneficiaries themselves contribute to the extension of development for their own benefit and reduction in development costs.

People's participation is the process in which individuals and families assure responsibility and act as an agent for their own development. People's participation will serve some of the basic needs for development as indicated below :

1. Create will and determination among people to improve their standard of life.
2. Identify and develop local resources to generate wealth for them.
3. Mobilise human and social resources for productive and meaningful purposes.
4. Create awakenness for development of community in various fields of potentials.
5. Arrange training for understanding new technologies.
6. Organise various fuctional groups, clubs of youths and women for leadership, skill training, environmental consciousness, reduction of drudgery in work, fight for their rights etc.
7. Provide open forum to discuss their problem and find indigenous economic and efficient solutions.
8. Encourage people to develop confidence, self-reliance instead of depending upon the government etc.

So it is through informing, motivating and encouraging the people that we can best hope to improve their living conditions. We should remember that the knowledge of the people is more valuable and useful than the wide general knowledge. A plan which does not take into account their perceptions, aspirations and preferences can have no operational validity.

Understanding about the community itself is the first pre-requisite of participation management followed by identification of problems, analysis and prioritization of needs, design of programmes and implementation of relevant and feasible design through formal and informal channels with local leader, NGOs and local organizations. The ultimate purpose is to encourage the people to run the programmes independently for their own benefit without others help. This will bring a sense of confidence and responsibility to take up development programmes. At the initial stage the people will face some problems which require guidance and monitoring to sort out such problems.

There are three sectors to manage the developmental works : State, the first sector is diminishing in economy. The second one is profit motivated private sector which is less concerned with rural development though some amount of money is spent for social development in selected cases. The third sector is NGOs and local institutions which have special significance and capabilities to be fully utilized for state policy implementation, mass propaganda and awareness. As NGOs have arisen out of voluntary impulse of charity upon which the social work practitioners have built up their theory and practice, they have found an honourable place in social work agenda. NGOs are catalysts and driving force of a society. NGOs play a critical role in promoting people's participative ability at village level, facilitate promotion of apex level organizations at block and district levels, educate people and create a favourable environment for interface. NGOs will have dominating role as the facilitator in the socio-political and economic development. There are a number of examples of commendable works conducted by capable and genuine NGOs in the country. Bureau of Integrated Rural Development (BIRD) an NGO from Assam (formed by persons retired from senior position of AAU and State Government having expertise and experiences in rural development technology) could raise the production of crops two or three times in many areas through people's participation. National Forest Policy now ensures as in Gujarat that local people participate in decisions relating to managing their forests. So the state policy should be to capitalize NGO sector and complementary relationship should grow up with market institutions. NGOs can mobilize local resources with external fund, involve in rural development, growth and social justice with people's participation.

The real issue of development is realization of the fact that, it is both materialistic and spiritual. Through participatory approach in various fields community empowerment will increase and farmers will gain faith in themselves for management of their own affairs. This will solve many problems and evils still standing in the way of development of economy and save the nature from destruction. Thus a creative option through people's participation as the key to rural development and poverty alleviation needs to be explored. Poor people's realities must figure high in the programmes which will gain meaning. It is the time to change policies to stretch heart and mind to the poor and neglected people, understand their problems and realities, rebuild the people's confidence and solve these through their participation surpassing all the complexities that may arise. It is possible through renewal of our mind.

18

ENLISTING PEOPLE'S PARTICIPATION IN SOIL CONSERVATION AND WATERSHED MANAGEMENT PROGRAMMES IN NORTH-EASTERN REGION

K. K. Satapathy

Introduction

Hilly watersheds of North-Eastern Region dominated by tribal population and characterised by poverty, lack of awareness and resource crunch impose total dependence on available resources which are diminishing and depleting at an alarming rate. Owing to preponderance of forests and barren and uncultivated lands, per capita availability of land for cultivation in the hill areas is lower than the all-India average; cultivation has been extended to marginal lands through extensive deforestation and shifting cultivation resulting in low productivity and soil erosion. As a result the population in many heavily eroded areas is high and this has resulted in over exploitation of sloping lands. Despite the efforts of several government and non-government organisations to promote soil and water conservation, there was hardly any progress made over past few decades. Land and water resources are interactive parts of natural ecosystem and should be managed on a watershed basis. Integrated management of natural resources, namely soil, water, vegetation, man, animal and environment on watershed basis in a holistic approach is essential for optimising production of food, fodder, fuel, fibre, fruits, flower, fish etc. for overall development of the area and social uplift.

Watershed development projects have been taken up in North-Eastern region under different programmes launched by Government of India. A critical review of the programmes indicates that one of the major shortcomings of watershed development approach has been the lack of people's participation in the programmes. The existing top-down government extension organisations have limited success in halting watershed resource degradation. The NGOs involved in the field also have achieved very little success in implementing complex programmes like watershed management. New paradigms of stake holders participation, changed attitudes/behaviour of service providers (government functionaries), greater emphasis on social contents, resolution of conflicts and harmonisation of new technical knowledge are the key contents for meeting the new challenges of watershed development. Mobilisation of people or community participation at all levels of planning, implementation and monitoring is one of the pre-requisites in any soil conservation and watershed management programmes.

Technological Aspects

Watershed management encompasses all activities for the management, of natural resources in a watershed-agricultural management, agrosilvopastural management, soil and water conservation, land use management, gully control, stream banks protection, water harvesting and water management, social and community forestry, natural forest regeneration management, reforestation, other common property resources management, policies effecting watershed resources and the like. Hence watershed management is multi-objective and multi-sectoral. Scientists have developed appropriate technologies to find solutions to most problems relating to watershed treatment. They range from simple check dams to large percolation/irrigation tanks, from vegetative barriers to contour bunds. A new approach — SALT — which is a combination of mechanical and biological measures has been introduced recently. SALT is a agroforestry system in which mechanical measures are recommended only to supplement the biological conservation and not as a substitute for them. Watershed treatment/development plans are prepared for all the arable and non-arable lands and the drainage lines; all the forest lands, government and community lands and private lands can be taken up for development activities.

People's Participation

The soil conservation and watershed management programmes belong to farmers who live in the watershed and use the watershed resources to obtain their daily requirements for food, fodder and fuel wood. Active participatory roles of these farmers are essential for the success of soil conservation and sustained use and management of watershed resources. Although legislation exists to encourage grassroot participation in the planning process, in practice it is not fully effective. Government therefore has to rely on the top-down approach and emphasis on achievement of physical targets that are often insufficiently flexible to account for the needs of individual communities. Farmers consider numerous objectives when they slect soil conservation measures. Some of these objectives correspond to those of scientists, but others do not. The government department should adopt a participatory approach rather than thrusting the programme on the people. Recent studies have shown that in many regions SWC programmes has not been successful not due to lack of their concern about erosion but primarily because the design of recommended technologies has not been suitable for the small farmers. Community participation is essential for successful implementation as well as for the maintaining of community assets created under the project. Community mobilisation could also be viewed as an important mechanism through which the responsibilities of common property resources management could be transferred back effectively to the people, so that more productive, sustainable and equitable development is possible. Allocation of resources, based on a community approach, rather than on an individual one adds an element of sustenance to the development process. Participation begins in the initial stage of designing and planning through the implementation, monitoring and evaluation stages and lasts up to follow-up stage of continuous maintenance and benefit sharing among participating groups. The extent to which communities demonstrate their ability to work together and take collective decisions is an important dimension of participation in watershed development programmes. The farmers' contribution has several advantages: they develop a sense of ownership, which also leads to transparency and reduces financial burden on government. Experiences have shown that there is no universally accepted formula for people's participation which can be replicated in all development programmes. Various concepts and definitions of people's participation have been developed in order to suit the objectives of a particular development project.

Indigenous Technical Knowledge

One of the main problems with our past efforts in soil conservation and watershed management was the lack of input from the users or local people. Available resources can be put to their most efficient and sustainable use with location specific knowledge, which is best generated and interpreted locally. Past experience shows that a simple alternative method for on farm research and technology transfer might consist of first understanding farmers practice, perception and technical knowledge. The experience suggests that the collective indigenous ideas and self-generated interests of groups of beneficiary farmers are prerequisite to mobilise people's participation at initial stage. The village communities have evolved their own technologies and numerous practices based on local knowledge and materials which are cost effective, simple and easy to operate and repair, each attuned to the agro-ecological systems in which it is employed. Increasing numbers of agricultural researcher are working closely with farmers to understand and address farm level conditions that shape technology choice. Along with the introduction of innovative technologies, the use of indigenous knowledge and local innovations must be fostered and encouraged. Farmers have created many farming patterns including multi-layer agriculture, animal husbandry, farming systems and home gardens in order to maximise production. In the hill areas, several models of comprehensive management are practised. Planning forest trees on hill tops is a priority for controlling erosion and to improve ecological environment. In the middle slope fruit trees are grown. In the foothill, where the slope is gentle, the soil is rich and water sources are plentiful, farm lands are developed by constructing ponds and check dams; aquatic production is developed in waterbodies. Such comprehensive management integrates long term benefits with medium and short term ones. The possibilities of modifications to make their improvements acceptable by the people need to be explored. This can only happen when the extentionists become facilitators or promoters of farmers' organisation rather than continue to remain agents of technology transfer only. In that case farmers' organisations themselves should become the repositories of indigenous knowledge and help horizontal transfer of this and adopt improved technologies by farmer to farmer exchange.

Participatory Rural Appraisal

Rural communities in India have long suffered from a dependency syndrome, expecting government subsidies as a condition for acceptance of project inputs. Community spirit has declined and motivation for community management of common property resources is lacking; external pressure for speeding the process often posed a serious constraint. The PRA based planning and identification of entry points largely overcame these difficulties. In PRA, emphasis is placed on empowering local people to assume an active role in analysing problems and drawing up plans with outsiders mainly acting as "facilitators". Farmers identify, define and articulate village situations as starting points. Their knowledge, skills and experience are respected and appreciated. Watershed team should use different participatory techniques like social mapping, transacts, time line analysis etc. together with first-hand information about the village community, the watershed, problems and achievements. Gathering information is only one of the objectives of PRA exercise. The more important objective is to interact with the village community in small groups to understand their perspectives, perception and priorities. The exercise provides chance to villagers to share their perception of problems and opportunities presented by the landscape. Participants become more aware of the opportunities and options. This ensures active and creative participation of the villagers in natural resource management. Instead of a top-down approach, a grassroot approach from the beginning of project formulation is desirable by establishing a dialogue with community leaders and discussing with them the tentative plans and options. The PRA exercise should lead to diagnosis of important problems and priorities. However, here it is no longer the external experts but rather the local people themselves who "own" the results of the study. These enable them to assume responsibility for implementing the activities based on them.

Sustainable Institutions

The self-organising capacities of communities and groups can be sustained only if suitable institutional mechanism is created. Various models of people's institutions have been functioning successfully in the country. Some villages have shown preference for the existing Gram Panchayats to take over all responsibilities for watershed activities. Other wished to create separate bodies for specific tasks, as they felt focus could be lost in a Gram Panchayat that is already preoccupied with government schemes. Gramsabhas are specially helpful in overcoming long misunderstanding and bridging communication gaps. Some hamlets preferred self help groups, because they felt that as the hamlet is remote from the main village, these would increase the likelihood of frequent and intensive interaction. Local institutions are important for mobilising resources and regulating their use with a view to maintain a long term base for productive activities. In the absence of local institutions, all conflicts are dealt with at higher level, yielding slower and often less appropriate outcomes. Local institutions encourage people to take a long time view by creating common expectation and a basis for co-operation that goes beyond individual interests. Local institutions carry a legitimacy, so people comply without inducements and sanctions. Although most indigenous measures, such as field bunds, waste weirs, waterways etc. require limited group action (cooperation among only neighbouring farmers), sometimes even this becomes difficult to achieve due to personal, social and other reasons. For effective implementation of different beneficiaries oriented programmes such as those under household production systems, well defined watershed level institutional framework and suitable guidelines should be provided as those of NWDPRA for the formation of Mitra Kishan Medal, self help groups and thrift group etc.

The unbrella of local institutions consist of institutions at three tiers :

(a) *Group level :* It may be persons in a small residential area like a neighbourhood or an occupational, age, gender, ethnic or other grouping. User groups, self help groups etc. at micro watershed level are the lowest tier of local institutions.

(b) *Community level :* Watershed development committee and watershed associations are second tier local institutions in watershed areas. The fact that people know each other, creates opportunities of collective and natural assistance for mobilising and managing resources on a self-directed and self-sustaining basis.

(c) *Localities level :* It may be extended to block levels. Project implementing agency or multi-disciplinary team in watershed comes in this tier.

Structure of such people's organisation and mode of selection of active members etc. should preferably be developed through adequate consultations amongst and with the people. The basic function of such committee besides offering a forum to interact with external agencies interested in supporting development works should be to form and implement collective desisions on matters related to watershed management and resolve conflicts locally and democratically. The watershed societies should be formalised and preferably be registered under an appropriate act of government.

Training

Massive awareness programmes need to be organised to make the farmers and farm women aware of the evil effcts of *Jhuming* and the scope for its replacement. Such programmes should be specially developed for village heads, clan chiefs, farmers and farm women, who are important agents in decision making. The village level institutions will be able to plan their development only if villagers have been trained for the tasks and in sufficient number. The experience of village development boards in Nagaland has shown that training a few people can lead to new power centre in the villages. As far as possible 1 to 2 persons from each village should be trained who can work as bare foot village extension workers and can liaison between government agencies and the village level bodies. For watershed users, training should be given in the technical aspects of *in situ* soil and moisture conservation techniques, operation and maintenance of community/individual civil works, agriculture, horticulture, social forestry, plantation techniques, raising community/individual nurseries, dairying and livestock management and other land uses etc., maintenance of accounts and procedures for extension of civil works and the like. Fields days and study tours are some of the extension approaches used to enhance adoption of improved techniques by the farmers.

Economic Issues

Few important policy issues concerning soil and water conservation investments relate to land tenure laws, institutional credit policies, land distribution programmes and policies to encourage particular type of land use. From the farmers' view points, lack of finance and profitabilities are the main constraints to adoption of soil and water conservation measures. Investments made by the Central and State governments are used to meet the material cost — seeds, seedlings, construction materials etc. whereas labour costs are shared by beneficiaries themselves. Farmers, however, are not interested in long term gains from any project and are not willing to sacrifice especially if they are living on the margin of subsistence. Actual experience proves that soil erosion control measures will raise the farmers standard of living above the poverty level if soil and water conservation activities are closely connected with economic benefit of the farmers. Production from conservation activities should become commodities, which can be marketed in future. Long and short term conservation measures needs to be well co-oriented. Short-term benefits encourage participation easily. The profits gained from short-term measures can be partially used to support engineering and vegetative measures. For example, the plantation of grasses, shrubs, and trees requires coordination of short, medium and long term measures. When tree species for plantation are selected, these should include trees aiding both conservation and economic value, which include both fast and slow growing trees. These result into ecological benefits being closely associated with production. User contribution to all engineering activities in the form of labour, would develop a sense of ownership and would help generate people's participation in the follow-up and maintenance of complete works.

Role of NGOs

Non-governmental organisation can play a very substantial role in protection activities and are better oriented to enlist people's participation. They have necessary skills and patience to work with people, to motivate them and to train them and thereby to empower them so that they can identify their problems and resolve them on their own eventually. Majority of the NGOs have social development goals as their primary objectives, viz. environment protection, employment generation etc. and receives assistance from national and international agencies. The role of non-governmental organisation (NGO) is also being recognised currently by the government even if grudgingly. At the same time NGOs are also beginning to realize the importance of coalition building with government for development rather than confrontation path.

REFERENCES

Rajora, R. (1998). *Integrated Watershed Management, Field Manual for Equitable Productive and Sustainable Development,* Rawat Publications, Jaipur.

Schreier, H., Shah, P. B. and Brown, S. (1995). Challenges in Mountain Resource Management in Nepal, *Proceedings of the Workshop held in Kathmandu,* Nepal 10-12 April, *1995.*

Sharma, P.N. and Wagle, M.P. (1995). *The Status of Watershed Management in Asia, Watershed Management in Tropics and Upper Himalayas.* Farmer Centred Agriculture Research Management (FARM) programme, Kathmandu, Nepal.

Tideman, E. M. (1996). *Watershed Management-guidelines for Indian Conditions.* Omega Scientific Publishers, New Delhi.

INDEX